WEIGHED
and
found
WANTING

*The Toronto experience examined
in the light of the Bible*

Bill Randles

Acknowledgements

Extracts from the Authorized Version of the Bible (The King James Bible), the rights in which are vested in the Crown, are reproduced by permission of the Crown's patentee, Cambridge University Press.

This edition published in Great Britain
by St Matthew Publications 1995
Second edition 1996
24 Geldart St, CAMBRIDGE CB1 2LX UK
+1223 363545 *fax: +1223 512304*

© Bill Randles
3336 Prairie Drive NE
Cedar Rapids, IA 52402
+319 366 0884 *Fax +319 366 5192*

ISBN 0 9524672 0 8

Printed & bound byOAK TREE PRESS, Eye, Suffolk IP21 5ST 01379 388888
Cover printed by CREDO PRINT Cambridge

Dedication

This book is dedicated to Traverse and Jewel Van der Merwe, who have faithfully sounded the alarm in spite of much rejection, hardship, and personal cost. Though Traverse has gone to be with the Lord, his legacy shall live on through the many who have been awakened to discern the times. This book can be largely attributed to the encouragement and input both Jewel and Traverse have given me.

Maranatha, O Come Lord Jesus!

Editor's Note for the English Edition

In editing **Weighed and found Wanting**, I have merely changed the American spellings but otherwise made very few alterations. I am most grateful to Pastor Bill Randles for permitting his book to be available in this English edition. His concern and prayer in writing this book has always been, "May God allow us to 'snatch some out of the fire.'"

The importance of this book in view of the present situation in the British churches cannot be overestimated.

Philip Foster

Contents

Introduction

Jude 24-25 Now unto him that is able to keep you from falling, and to present you faultless before the presence of his glory with exceeding joy, to the only wise God our Saviour, be glory and majesty, dominion and power, both now and ever. Amen.

My name is Bill Randles and I am a Pentecostal pastor, who is very concerned about the direction the church is taking these days, especially the Pentecostal/Charismatic expression of the church. The scriptures repeatedly warn of a huge departure from the faith which was once and for all delivered unto us by the apostles. They speak of a day when men would be swept away from faith in God by a tremendous delusion. Even more amazing, is the fact that the source of that delusion would be God Himself, as a judgement on those who wouldn't "receive the love of the truth." The time has now come for those of us who have considered ourselves to be "spirit filled" and "full Gospel" and in some cases, even "cutting edge" Christians, to begin to take these warnings seriously. Who do we think we are, anyway? Are we above deception? Are the biblical warnings of the delusion only applicable to those in obvious cults, like Mormons and Jehovah's Witnesses, or are they for the elect?

Why I Write

The current "renewal" or "revival" that is being promoted by people like Rodney Howard Browne, the Toronto Airport Vineyard, and others, actually has the potential of taking people's eyes off of the God of the Bible and turning them to sensual manifestations and mystical experiences. Unless some leadership is offered and discernment is applied, I predict that many of God's people will be hurt, disillusioned and even made shipwreck of their faith, as a result of this "Mystical Revival." And to make matters even worse, all too many shepherds and leaders do not know whether to join, oppose, or ignore the growing movement. This lack of confident principled leadership has thrown God's flocks into much consternation. Many high profile ministries have endorsed this move. Unfortunately, peer pressure will sweep in many of the undecided. This book is written to challenge some of the prevailing notions, and to offer a different perspective to the public discussion. It is our desire to stimulate afresh, the vigorous Berean spirit (Acts 17) in the family of God!

After all it would be bad enough if it was the believers alone who were hurt by these false revivals and false moves of the Spirit. But sinners also are going to be hurt on two different levels. There are those sinners who look at the world as it is, aching, crying, in pain, suffering and confusion, and then look at this expression of the church, laughing hysterically, "partying in the Lord," acting unreasonably, even drunkenly, and they will rule the church out entirely as a relevant, compassionate witness of truth. Unfortunately, they will also rule out the Christ and the Gospel which the church is representing. They will be heard saying, "These people don't care, they are in their own world, they themselves are merely escaping from the harsh realities of this hurting world. Where is Christ in all of this?" There is a huge difference between being scandalized by the foolishness of the cross, and scandalized by people roaring like lions, going into trances and laughing ridiculously through sermons on the judgement of God!

Even worse than the first level of harm is the second. How could anything the church does be worse than "turning people off" by a misrepresentation of Jesus? The only thing worse, would be to inoculate sinners to the Gospel, by giving them an artificial salvation experience. There are many who will make false conversions as a result of being "touched by the Spirit." The laughing, hilarious, drunkenness promoting "Jesus" of these meetings is definitely not the Jesus of the Holy Scriptures. In this way, many are being inoculated against true Christianity. They have had their "shot" of Jesus and the new wine, they don't need anymore. They especially don't need anything from any "dead or religious" churches. (Translate that, non-entertaining)! Let me repeat, the Jesus of spiritual drunkenness is not the Jesus of the Bible!

Roots of the Renewal

This sensual revival has not just suddenly appeared out of the blue, however. Nor have these occurrences spontaneously burst out within the past year, as some would suggest. The idea that many have, is that it is like Pentecost which, **suddenly**, came with a rushing mighty wind. In the same way, people are being empowered by this intoxicating spirit. Rather, I would like to demonstrate for you that people have been preconditioned for this "move" for at least 40 years now, whether those involved realize it or not.

The true roots of this revival go back to the now discredited New Order of the Latter Rain and Manifested Sons of God movement of the late 1940s and 1950s. Though the Assemblies of God denounced these movements as heretical then, they seem to have had a resiliency. The ideas that they have spawned have continually cropped up over the years, perhaps with different emphases or diverse names for concepts, but holding virtually the same erroneous premises. One of those premises has been that the church should quit hoping and looking forward to the rapture (the physical return of Jesus Christ to rescue us from this world and complete our salvation). Instead they believe that we should get on with the business of ruling and reigning over this world, and in a very real sense, we are to complete our own salvation. The emphasis has subtly shifted from Christ to us. **We** are supposedly the ones who are to evolve into a "great end times army that will put God's enemies under our feet," **we** are supposedly the ones to whom God said, "Ask of me and I will give you the heathen for your inheritance." In short, the church either replaces Christ or "is THE Christ." Whether the movement calls itself the Latter Rain Movement, the Manifested Sons, Kingdom Now, Dominion Theology, Restorationism, The Faith Movement, or the Third Wave, all have either come to or been based on this erroneous conclusion.

The hope has shifted. Through bold teachers, "prophets," and "apostles," and their "words," the old idea of wanting Jesus to come back quickly to complete our redemption has been scoffed at as "escapist," "irresponsible," and "religious." Instead of that, the new hope is, for the time when the church would come into her own, be perfected by restored apostles and prophets and would enter into the "Latter Rain," the greatest revival ever seen or experienced. This is what people are looking for. If Jesus came back now, He would interrupt the "progress" that the church is making. We are actually told that He can't come back yet anyway, for the Lord's coming back for a perfectly united and unblemished church. (Actually, Eph 5 teaches that *He will present to Himself* a church *without spot or wrinkle*.) Could this laughing revival be the long awaited "Great End Times Revival," "The Feast of the Tabernacles," or "The Latter Rain?" As you will see, these are some of the names now given for the new hope, which replaces the former hope: The coming of Jesus.

All of this has an appeal, for what Christian wouldn't want a "great end times revival" that will sweep all nations? But the fact that it all sounds good doesn't mean that it is of God. The real question we should ask is, what do the scriptures lead us to expect in the Last Days? That is all that truly matters. Do we hear the apostles preparing people for the ultimate expression of the church, or for an apostasy? Will whole nations be swept in to the kingdom of God, or will all nations actually "hate you for my (Jesus) name's sake?" The revival concept is wonderful and there always can be and will be localized awakenings and revivings of God's people, wherever they obey II Chronicles 7:14. However, in scripture we are told to expect apostasy, deception, and a universal revival of "lying signs and wonders." We do not read of a Christian domination of the world! The only way to come to this erroneous conclusion is to use replacement theology, in which all the scriptures pertaining to Israel are re-applied to the church!

One concept underlying all of this mystical revival is experience over doctrine, in seeking the knowledge of God. Taking their cue from this wicked and perverted generation, too many spiritual leaders show a disdain for dogma, or teaching, as being cold, dead, or restrictive. The new authentication is experience. People are being lured into trying to "feel God," and "know Him intimately." Words like "passion," "abandonment" and "radical love affair with Jesus" are being held up as viable options, as opposed to cold, dead, "head knowledge" of God. Over and over again we are told by the likes of Rodney Howard Browne, "turn off your mind," "get out of your head" and enter in. "Come drink at Joel's place, what'll you have?" flows the seduction. Those who would question all of this are castigated as "religious deadheads," "mainlining on prunes and sucking lemons." These "apostles and prophets," never miss an opportunity to mock those who don't "enter in" and "drink at Joel's place."

Open Call to Shepherds

After you read the book, you'll have some choices to make. Which way will you go? Will you rise up and offer your people some principled direction? I pity the rank and file, non-ministerial, uninformed member of the Body. So many "waves" to ride. How is one supposed to know? The Christian media seem to endorse this, and so do many high powered ministries. If God's people need anything at all these days, it's principled leadership. The book of Isaiah says, When the enemy comes in like a flood, the Lord will lift up a standard against him. But as Psalm 94:16 asks, *Who will rise up with me against the evildoers?* Pastor, you might be saying right now, "I just preach the truth, I never come against error." That would be great, if you were the only one preaching. With **Trinity Broadcasting Network**, **Christian Broadcasting Network**, and **Charisma Magazine** and a host of other sources, error is having a field day these days! Never has the scripture been so easily fulfilled,

> **II Timothy 3:6-7** *For of this sort are they which creep into houses, and lead captive silly women laden with sins, led away with divers lusts, ever learning, and never able to come to the knowledge of the truth.*

As I said earlier, I'm writing as a pastor with a pastoral burden on my heart. I pioneered Believers in Grace Fellowship in Cedar Rapids, Iowa back in 1982. We are a small, tightly knit, loving community of faith. I love this church and if I wasn't pastor, I'd go here anyway, for here I have found "koinonia" in the truest sense. As I have told this congregation many times, "I'd rather meet with 10 people who seriously follow Jesus, than 350 half baked ones looking for the next wave." I guarantee you the Christians I pastor are serious about "faith in Jesus and love for the saints" and the hope of His coming!

Not only am I a Pentecostal pastor, I am a recent author of a book called **Making War in the Heavenlies...A Different Look at Spiritual Warfare**. In which I attempt to call attention to error in that particular field, and give once again the orthodox view of spiritual warfare.

On a more fundamental level, I am a Christian, a husband, a father and I love the Lord Jesus and marvel at His grace and mercy. I love Him because I found out, He loved me first. It pleased God to reveal His Son in me in 1977, and it was also that year that I was endowed with power from on high to be His witness. I have a lovely wife, Kristin, and four lovely children, a son-in-law and a grandson. My wife is my best friend and I wouldn't be the man I am today, had God not given her to me. My daughter, Dara, is 22, married to William and they have given us a grandson, Abraham. My next daughter, Anna, is 12 and my sons are Samuel, 5 and Marcus, 2, and they bring me much joy. I am a rich man!

Well, there you have it. Who I am and why I write. Let's pray. Father, in the precious name of Jesus, who is the true shepherd and bishop of our souls, give the reader of this book a spirit of wisdom and revelation in the knowledge of you, and let the eyes of our understanding be flooded with light, to know what is of you and what isn't of you. Help us to stay charitable in our assessment of these things. To be willing to have a love that discerns. Deliver your people from the ravages of heresy and delusion by giving them two things. One, a love for the truth and two, shepherds after your own heart to feed them both wisdom and knowledge. Let shepherds receive clarity in these foggy times that there may be light houses, standards everywhere, for the floods have lifted up Oh, Lord, but we are confident that the voice of the Lord is more than the sound of many waters, in Jesus' name, Amen!

The grace of our Lord Jesus Christ be with your Spirit—Amen!

1
What's Going on in Toronto?

Canadian Broadcasting's "Sunday Morning" radio program recently broadcast a story on a newsworthy event in Toronto. This was very helpful because when trying to describe the "Toronto Blessing" to a congregation in Michigan, I could tell I was stretching the borders of my own credibility. The congregation had a hard time believing that tens of thousands of people were coming from all over the world to a little church in Toronto, to "get touched" by the Spirit, laugh uncontrollably, roar like lions, be paralysed, and shake violently. I could see that look of disbelief on their eyes, but was relieved when two ladies made it known to the congregation that they were from Toronto, and yes, it's all true and even more. They then produced a taped segment of CBC's "Sunday Morning." The following are some of the quotes, (interspersed by moaning, laughter of an unnatural nature, and prayer in tongues).

Planes land every few minutes at Toronto's Pearson Airport, right over the top of Toronto's Vineyard Church. There are over 600 Vineyard Churches around the world, but the Toronto branch has such a direct line to the Holy Spirit, some 40,000 people from around the world have flown in to "do carpet time," giggle with "The Holy One," and speak in tongues. Staid and more established churches have been looking on with alarm and jealousy, and if they aren't jazzing up their own services, they are denouncing the airport church as the work of the devil.

Now keep in mind that this is a secular news program. It doesn't seem plausible that the Airport Vineyard would ever say that they have a special line to the Holy Spirit, nor do I know of them referring to "giggling with the Holy One."

However, the radio report was incredible. The maniacal laughter in the background, was mixed with common worship songs, moans, crying and some shrieking. The reporter in a hushed, reverent voice says:

A young woman is lying on the floor with her eyes closed, as she speaks her body jerks ever so slightly. All around her people are laughing or crying or shaking uncontrollably...[In the background is maniacal, forced, shrill laughter]...This is what the Vineyard Church calls the Holy Spirit's joy of laughter. They aren't laughing at anything being said, they are just laughing...

Toward the end of the radio program, shivers ran down my spine when I heard a deep, throaty, growl; of a woman, "prophesying" in what sounded like a lion's voice, "I will rescue my children, I will go after them and I, I will rescue them..."

What is Going on in Toronto?

2
The Secular Press Drew My Attention To It

My interest in the subject of the "Toronto Blessing" first began after reading a **Time Magazine** article entitled, "Laughing for the Lord." The article was primarily about "revivalist fervour" invading the Church of England. The Anglican Church, as it is also known, being what it is, has never been known for fervour of any kind, at least not in a long time, so the recent happenings there are newsworthy. This is a description of a typical service at Holy Trinity Brompton Church in London.

Though pathetically tiny flocks of Londoners attend many Anglican services, Holy Trinity Brompton has a standing room only turnout of 1,500. Oblivious to the hot, airless sanctuary, the youthful throng buzzes with an anticipation more common at a rock concert or a rugby match. After the usual scripture readings, prayers, and singing, the chairs are cleared away. Curate Nickey Gumbel prays that the Holy Spirit will come upon the congregation. Soon, a woman begins laughing. Others gradually join her with hearty belly laughs. A young worshipper falls to the floor, hands twitching. Another falls, then another and another. Within half an hour, there are bodies everywhere as supplicants sob, shake, roar like lions, and strangest of all, laugh uncontrollably.[1]

The article in **Time** called this phenomenon, "The Toronto Blessing." This is what drew my attention to Toronto. There are many other articles in both secular and Christian publications describing similar church situations in the United States, United Kingdom, Australia, and other places. They are all acknowledging Toronto as the catalyst. The **Time Magazine** article also linked the "Laughing Revival" to the ministry of Rodney Howard Browne who, as you will see, plays a pivotal role in what has happened in Toronto. A later chapter will be devoted to Rodney Howard Browne, and the impact of his ministry.

Another secular publication which mentions this manifestation is the British paper, **The Daily Mail**. In the "femail" section of Friday, September 2, 1994, an article was entitled, "This man has been given the Toronto Blessing. What in God's name is going on?" Allow me to give you a few excerpts from the article,

It is, it must be said, a disquieting sight: The congregation fall where they stand. Others weep uncontrollably. Many shake violently as though having a fit. Visions of angels, huge figures, some with wings, bathed in orange light swim before their eyes. This is the Toronto Blessing...In Britain, no one has espoused the Toronto effect more enthusiastically then the Rt. Rev. David Pytches. [Pytches may be remembered for writing Some Said It Thundered, a defence of the Kansas City Prophets] Pytches, an evangelical, Charismatic enthusiast was one of the first to visit Toronto. He and his wife Mary came back and reported to the Church of England's Holy Trinity Brompton...In recent weeks, hundreds of their large congregation of nearly a thousand have been falling and laughing, groaning, and weeping, barking and making other animal noises. Some roar like lions which may have something to do with the biblical passage that Mary Pytches frequently mentions in connection with the Toronto Blessing—Hosea 11: *They will follow the Lord; He will roar like a lion. When He roars, His children will come trembling.* It was on her visit to Toronto that Mary Pytches heard the roaring and found herself wailing...[2]

The article goes on to describe the national and even international impact of the experience, and makes the connection to it with the teachings of John Wimber. Then toward the end, the writer makes this insightful observation,

The difference between the present movement and revivals of the 18th century is that the latter were characterized by powerful preaching, a strong sense of self loathing and of repentance, none of which is a feature of the Toronto Blessing or the Charismatic movement from which it came.[3]

The Christian Media Coverage of Toronto

The June, 1994 issue of **Charisma**, in an article entitled, "Renewal Excites Canadian Churches," described in a strikingly similar way as the secular press, a typical service in the Toronto Airport Vineyard.

The meetings are wildly pentecostal in style, not the type of worship services that normally attract dignified theologians or staid denominational leaders. On a typical evening, dozens of people can be found lying or rolling on the floor, many of them laughing uncontrollably. Many of the participants testify of being healed of sickness or delivered of emotional problems.[4]

However, **Charisma** reports that the leaders of the Toronto renewal do not consider themselves to be in a revival in the classic sense of the term. According to **Charisma**, John Arnott, Pastor of Airport Vineyard told them that exuberant joy is a characteristic of the first phase of revival, but true revival ultimately impacts thousands of unsaved. At this point, the Toronto Renewal has primarily touched Christians. Another Christian publication, a magazine in the United Kingdom, called **Alpha** wrote a piece in their July 1994 edition that discussed this called, "Rumours of Revival." Dave Roberts describes the Toronto meetings as, "characterised by literally dozens of people falling "under the power" and laughing uncontrollably. Consistent reports from around the world talk of a state similar to drunkenness, with those affected losing control of their limbs and having to be carried out to cars for their journey home."[5]

This same article quotes another magazine, **Redemption**, as saying,
A hallmark of this revival is the emphasis on worship and praise. Missionaries report

that the Shekinah glory of the Lord seems to descend on the meetings...The emphasis is on holiness, the desire of the people to praise and worship and the increase in concern for reaching others is genuine.[6]

There is a glowing article called "Spreading Like Wildfire" written by Eleanor Mumford for **Renewal Magazine**, July, 1994. Mrs. Mumford is the wife of John Mumford, Senior Pastor of a Vineyard Church in London. She writes:

I have just been on a trip to a church in Toronto. A Baptist pastor who is increasingly involved in what is going on there has written, "There has come a notable renewal and revival of hope, faith and expectation. The spirit of God has been pouring out freedom, joy, and power"...With all this has come a renewing of commitment and a rekindled passion for Jesus and the work of the kingdom...

Mrs. Mumford followed this quote with a glowing personal report of the Toronto Blessing and its impact on her,

I went to Toronto because I have never been slow to go to a party. I also went because I knew I was spiritually bankrupt and I went with tremendous expectancy...There was a beauty on those who were ministering there...These were men and women who had spent 130 days in the company of Jesus. Like Stephen, their faces shone. I saw the power of God poured out in an incredible measure...People are getting freed, and getting healed...Jesus is restoring His joy and His laughter is like medicine to my soul...Jesus is breaking down the barriers of His church...For myself there is a greater love for Jesus than I've ever known, a greater excitement about the kingdom than I ever thought possible.[7] [8] [9]

Something significant is happening and it has the potential to have a huge worldwide impact. This phenomenon won't leave people neutral, for either they will love and appreciate it or distrust and criticize it. The time has come upon us, particularly we who are Charismatic/Pentecostal Christians, when we would be forced to decide what we actually believe. Unfortunately that kind of decision divides. It is hard to find any fault with any experience which causes people to "love Jesus," be set free, or releases the joy of the Lord. Those are the very things I have dedicated my life to. However, we cannot just look at a movement pragmatically and judge its validity solely on the basis of "results." We hear, "Well, it works, it made me love Jesus, it must be of God!" Just because something "works" it doesn't mean that it is of God. In other words, the end doesn't necessarily justify the means. We must look at the principles, the premises underlying any movement at all, in order to even begin to make an objective evaluation. Remember, our Lord told us to *Judge all things and hold fast to that which is good.* Dare I be the "bad guy" and challenge you to take another, critical look at the "Laughing Revival?" Well, someone has to sooner or later. After all, what do you mean, you have a greater passion for Jesus?

How It All Started In Toronto

The Vineyard itself has been helpful in researching the brief history of this renewal. They have readily made papers available in an attempt to give people a framework in which to interpret what they believe God is doing in their midst. There is a helpful publication entitled "What in the World is Happening to Us?" by Bill Jackson of the Champaign Illinois Vineyard Church. **Charisma** and **Renewal Magazine** also provide a summation of how it all started.

You can start to understand this renewal by looking at two men, Randy Clark and John Arnott. Randy pastors a Vineyard church in St. Louis and Arnott, the Airport Vineyard in Toronto. Both of them arrived separately at that state that every Christian and for sure every minister can relate to, dissatisfaction with where they were at and hunger for more of God. This is a good, though painful place to be, because I believe God uses it to press us in to seek Him all the more. Pastor Clark told **Charisma Magazine**, "I felt empty, powerless, and so little anointed, emotionally, spiritually, and physically. I knew I was burning out."[10]

In the summer of 1993, Clark talked with another minister, an associate who had sat under the ministry of Rodney Howard Browne. Clark's friend told of how he had been revived during the meeting! Again, according to **Charisma**, Clark said, "What my friend was describing—people shaking, falling, laughing—was what I'd seen many years earlier in the Vineyard revivals. I knew this was what I needed."[11] Take notice that it wasn't truth, but manifestations that led him to Rodney Howard Browne.

Clark decided to attend a meeting of Rodney Howard Browne's but balked when he found out Rodney Howard Browne would be in Tulsa, Oklahoma, at Kenneth Hagin Jr's Rhema Bible Church. Clark had theological problems with the Word Faith Movement. However, Clark said that the Lord reproved him for a smug attitude, saying, "You have a denominational Spirit, how badly do you want to be touched afresh?"[12] After setting aside his prejudices, Clark went to the meeting and was prayed for to receive a fresh infilling of the Holy Spirit. When he went back to his church, powerful manifestations began to occur.

In October, 1993, Randy Clark attended a regional meeting of Vineyard Churches in Wisconsin. There the overseer, Happy Leman, asked him to testify. As he did, "powerful demonstrations of God's power broke out at the meeting." Also, according to "What in the World is Happening to Us," another "Limited outbreak [occurred] at the Champaign Vineyard the following Saturday."[13]

John Arnott

Pastor John Arnott also had experienced a dissatisfaction and was sensing the need for a fresh anointing of the Spirit. His hunger for God's touch took him to Argentina, where he witnessed great spiritual revival, as well as attending the meetings of Benny Hinn. According to "What in the World is Happening to Us"

Happy Leman told Arnott the results of Randy Clark's ministry at the conference. Upon hearing this, Arnott arranged a meeting for Clark at his church in Toronto in January, 1994. The meeting was supposed to last less than a week, but instead, has continued to this day. They still meet six days a week. Tens of thousands from all over the world have come to Toronto to "soak" in the presence of God, to "get it" as they say and "get it" they do, taking "it" back to home churches all over the world! Many come to do "carpet time" "soaking" in the "presence of the Lord." Vineyard literature encourages "soaking" which is repeated reception of prayer and exposure to the "Spirit." "What in the World is Happening to Us" advises people in its preface to "Ask for more and more of His Spirit. Keep coming for more—keep drinking," and "Don't become discouraged if you do not receive as much as another does—keep asking for more."[14] In another document simply entitled "Toronto June 94 Thoughts" we are advised,

> Soaking in the Holy Spirit. It's okay to receive many times of prayer at the same meeting. It is also okay to receive prayer every time we gather. In fact, people seem to receive better and more fully, each successive time. [They relax to the idea]. The more the soaking, the deeper the impact. If you fall over, don't try to get up quickly, lie there and soak.[15]

Impartation

Impartation seems to be another significant word and I must say, it is impartation that I see as being one of the most alarming aspects of this. By impartation, I mean the ability to pass it on, usually by laying on of hands. This is the strongest and most alarming characteristic of Rodney Howard Browne and the Toronto Blessing. Mystical experiences are imparted to ministers who return to their churches and revel in this newly found mystical power. The Spirit that is working in this move, won't be limited to the laying on of hands either, many are "getting it" just standing in services, overcome by shaking, laughing, weeping, or whatever other irrational experience. They come out of the meeting dynamically transformed. The impartation is for change and people are changing! Does God change people in this way? There is no truth with which to conform to, just "BAM!" The Spirit hits you and you change? This could be possibly our judgement for discontent. Like the world—we want change—we are dissatisfied with the status quo. We want something to happen, anything. At times it seems, that the Word of God doesn't satisfy, we are hungry for quail. And God is giving it. Soon, it will be coming out of our noses. *Is it God?!*

A Lot of This is About Manifestations

A Baptist pastor in Canada, Guy Chevreau, who is a participant in this renewal, was quoted as saying,

"What we are talking about here is God's manifest presence, such that He is seen, felt and experienced and folks' lives are getting changed."[16] He went on to say about it, "It's redefining the church, reminding us that church shouldn't be boring," and describes the renewal as, "a party with the Lord."[17] There is an appeal to those who are discontented, who find that church is boring (?), it needs to be redefined (!?), we aren't lively enough. One of the chief weapons of the false teacher is the use of discontent. People have been conditioned to think that the "Book of Acts" church consisted of one miracle explosion after another and that there was perfect unity and love. They believe that the modern church falls short of that and actually needs to be redefined! The truth is that the church of the Book of Acts was assaulted with heresies and divisions, and the miracles took place over a period of 30 years. By contrast, this "renewal" isn't based on some particular truth being emphasized, but it is being described, qualified, and authenticated by sensuous manifestations, signs and wonders, and quite frankly, in many respects, it is a reaction to boredom!

As Pentecostals, we believe in and have experienced many miracles and divine interventions. We all long for revival and to see God move. We pray with Isaiah, *O that you would rend the heavens and come down, that the mountains would melt at your presence and that you would do terrible things we weren't expecting!* (Rough paraphrase of Isa 64:1).

But when discontent is appealed to time and again, such as "The church isn't united enough, doesn't love enough, is too hung up on doctrine, has head knowledge, but no intimacy and on and on ad nauseam..." eventually, that kind of preaching wears the church down and makes her more vulnerable to whatever new thing that comes along. False fire is offered to the Lord instead of patiently waiting on God for His fire. Who says the church isn't united, anyway? Every true believer is **already** in the unity of the Spirit. Anytime we get hyped into trying to manufacture what God already gave us (unity), we get further away from God's purpose.

Laughing

An obvious major manifestation associated with this revival is laughter. The laughter is being called "Holy laughter" and scriptures about laughter, such as Psalm 126, are being used to verify it. Also, scriptures about joy, in fact more scriptures about joy than laughter because there aren't that many positive scriptures about laughter. Most laughing scriptures are of the "Woe to you who laugh now," variety, or "they laughed him to scorn." The laughter that is exhibited in these revivals needs to be re-examined. In many cases it is interrupting laughter. Reports are coming from all over the world of how the preaching of the Word, communion, or worship are being disrupted by gales of irrational laughter. We are not talking about a laughter based on any particularly funny or humorous notion. There is an irrationality to this laughter, as well as an uncontrollable element to it.

Abandonment is a word that comes to my mind, people are abandoning their common senses, and their critical faculties and giving themselves over to this hilarity.

A pastor, Terry Virgo, describes a service which, presumably, he attended in England,

> As he read his opening remarks, the power of God swept through the building, totally unrelated to the words that he had said, which actually were rather serious and solemn. His opening remarks were, "The story of Solomon is one of the most tragic in the whole Bible," this sober comment was greeted by sudden outbursts of hilarious laughter...There was no way we could stop this spontaneous, uninvited laughter...The meeting continued until 11:30 at night with no opportunity for the speaker to preach.[18]

The "Spirit" which is compelling this seems to be saying, "All of that (preaching the Word of God) is totally irrelevant." Rodney Howard Browne boasts of preaching on hell and being almost drowned out by the laughter! One of Rodney Howard Browne's initiates, an Episcopal priest, likes to tell the story of how, after being "blessed" he went home to his Episcopal church and burst out laughing at the most solemn moment of the service, the consecration of the Eucharistic elements. No matter what you may think of liturgical services, any Christian knows that communion is no time for levity. But he ended up on the floor, laughing so hard! Could this be a mocking spirit? Sent to get us to count the Word of God and communion, and the fear of God, irrelevant? Is this what they mean when they say, "We are past all that (communion and preaching), we want to be intimate with God."

Involuntary Shaking and Other Weird Acts

Though this has been called by some a "laughing revival," laughter is by no means the only or even primary manifestation. The New Life Vineyard Fellowship, pastored by Wes Campbell, has produced what seems to be a newsletter called "Prophet Sharing." Mr. Campbell presented a segment entitled, "Why All the Shaking?" Campbell gives a number of scriptures that validate the phenomena. [It is true that we can "tremble before the Lord." Many times I have seen congregations literally shaking at the preaching of His Word. In God's actual Manifest Presence even the inanimate objects are shaken!] But Campbell doesn't stop at scripture, in Article II, he gives four General Reasons for the Shaking:[19]

1. To get our attention.
2. A form of anointing.
3. A visible representation on and in our flesh of what is happening in the spirit world.
4. It is God's sovereign way of choice.

God does want to get people's attention, He can do it in any way that it pleases Him. Regarding a form of anointing? According to scripture, we are anointed. Beware of anyone who wants to tell you that what you already have in Jesus isn't enough. The third is the most incredible and disturbing to me. Why? Because it is probably the best definition of the word **Mysticism** that I've seen in a long time! The attempt to interpret and interact with the spirit world through the flesh. An extremely dangerous practice, I might add, which opens you up to the spirit world.

Openness seems to be a highly valued character trait in this move. The paper, "Toronto June 94 Thoughts" advises you to:

IV.   Experience it before trying to analyze it. It's your spirit God is dealing with primarily. In fact, when you are under the anointing, your mind is very clear and aware of what's going on, and that can be a distraction to what He's doing in the Spirit. It does not invalidate the experience.

VII.   This is not so much a time of "getting stuff out," more of "getting stuff in." It is probably wise, initially, not to pray in tongues, or English a lot. (That's you ministering out). I found it helpful when I felt the Lord there to just breath in deeply and imagine I am inhaling the Spirit.[20]

Mike Bickle and Michael Sullivant have produced a paper entitled, "God's Manifest Presence, Understanding the Phenomena that Accompany the Spirit's Ministry." The Vineyard people seem to have a strong motivation to give people as much help as possible in interpreting what they consider to be the move of the Spirit. In a segment entitled "Catalogue of Manifestations" he tells us:

The Hebrew and Biblical model of the unity of personality implies that the Spirit affects the body. At times, the human spirit is so affected by the glory of God, the human body is not capable of containing the intensity of these spiritual encounters and strange physical behaviour results. Sometimes, though certainly not always, the bodily responses are human responses to the spirit's activity and not directly caused by the Holy Spirit. However, this does not imply that they are therefore carnal and should be forbidden. Following are phenomena that have been observed in contemporary experience: shaking, jerking, loss of bodily strength, heavy breathing, eyes fluttering, lips trembling, oil on the body, changes in skin colour, weeping, laughing, "drunkenness," staggering, travailing, dancing, falling, visions, hearing audibly into the spirit realm, inspired utterances—ie prophecy, tongues, interpretation, angelic visitations, and manifestations, jumping, violent rolling, screaming, wind, heat, electricity, coldness, nausea as discernment of evil, smelling or tasting good and evil presence, tingling, pain in body as discernment of illness, feeling heavy weight or lightness, trances, altered physical state while seeing into the spiritual world, inability to speak normally, disruption of natural realm, ie electrical circuits blown.[21]

What a list! What are we supposed to do with that? Are they saying that these might be the body's response to God at times, or that they could be the direct activity of God at other times? What about some of them being symptoms of demonization? For instance, electrical circuits being blown (poltergeist, as it is known in some circles). I realize that at one time, that particular phenomena was considered a confirming sign to the ministry of a certain Kansas City Prophet, but I can't believe that it is an example of "the human response to God," nor do I believe that God is blowing fuses just to let us know He is here! A closer look at much of the above mentioned list is more like a description of classic demonization than it is a catalogue of manifestation of the Spirit of God.

Mike Bickle is not, to my knowledge, directly related to the "Toronto Blessing." He is, no doubt, a part of the supporting influence, as a fellow Vineyard pastor. He wrote this paper in the spring of 1994 to explain "widespread occurrences of the manifestations of the Holy Spirit across the United States and Canada."[22] No doubt, to give the Body of Christ a theological framework from which to interpret this renewal. Bickle is however, in my opinion, responsible for contributing to the preconditioning necessary to open people up to this phenomena. How? By promoting the infamous Kansas City Prophets. I'll elaborate on that ahead.

Spiritual Drunkenness

A major phenomena associated with and even promoted by this revival, is spiritual drunkenness. "We are partying with God now,"[23] according to "What in the World is Happening to Us." The joy of salvation is being subtly reinterpreted along this line:

> In the early days of the apostles, as they were searching for a word that would communicate to the Gentiles the ecstasy in having their sins forgiven and being in right relationship with God through the atoning blood of Christ Jesus, they chose the word evangelion, which we now translate, "gospel" or "good news." It was a completely secular word that was used in reference to the emperor's birthday. It was a holiday, a day of good news. The apostles travelled through the ancient world preaching that the day of God's party had come...We are learning to party in God again...[24]

The fallacies of this kind of thing should be obvious to all. The apostles weren't ever in the position of trying to find the right word for the message of God, to communicate to the Gentiles. The word gospel came from Jesus Himself. Furthermore, read the apostle's sermons, they proclaimed Jesus as Lord and called for repentance, not, "God's party has come!" But it sounds so good to a generation who have been conditioned already to see the things of God through such "fun-loving" glasses. After all, if it's not "fun" it will never sell! No doubt this sensuous theology will have a great appeal to certain segments of the population. Were the disciples spiritually drunk on Pentecost? At least one Vineyard document thinks so:

> They [the disciples] would not be accused of being drunk because they were speaking in different languages. They would be accused of such because they were acting like

drunks, ie laughing, falling, slurred speech by some, boldness through lack of restraint, etc.[25]

What can we expect though, when you consider the source of this movement? Remember, it was passed on to Randy Clark and eventually John Arnott through the ministry of Rodney Howard Browne! This is the man who delights in calling himself, "God's Bartender," invites people to come and drink at "Joel's Place" and promotes spiritual drunkenness.

We have all heard the cute testimony in Charismatic circles, "I used to have to get drunk to drown my sorrows, but now that I'm saved, I have the new wine, and I have no sorrows, I feel better now than ever. It's free and it doesn't leave me hung over!" This usually brings a hearty laugh. Is spiritual drunkenness a good thing? How are we to interpret this phenomena? Does Acts 2 or Eph 5:18 teach that the disciples got drunk in the spirit? It was the mockers who suggested that they were drunk, to which Peter immediately replied, *These men are not drunk as you suppose*...Eph 5:18 is a straightforward command to be not drunk with wine, because of excess, instead be filled with the Spirit! The Biblical admonition is to be sober, alert, watchful, not abandoned, or ecstatic.

Spiritual Drunkenness in the Bible

This is not to say that spiritual drunkenness is an unscriptural phenomena, for the Word of God does acknowledge the reality of such an experience. However, according to the prophets, spiritual drunkenness is to be viewed more as a judgement of God than as a blessing. It is a judgement on an apostate people, a people who are full of worship, *This people draws near to me with their lips, but are far from me with their heart.*

Isaiah 29:9-14 Stay yourselves, and wonder; cry ye out, and cry: they are drunken, but not with wine; they stagger, but not with strong drink. For the Lord hath poured out upon you the spirit of deep sleep, and hath closed your eyes; the prophets and your rulers, the seers hath he covered. And the vision of all is become unto you as the words of a book that is sealed, which men deliver to one that is learned, saying, Read this, I pray thee; and he saith, I cannot; for it is sealed: and the book is delivered to him that is not learned, saying, Read this, I pray thee: and he saith, I am not learned. Wherefore the Lord said, Forasmuch as this people draw near me with their mouth, and with their lips do honour me, but have removed their heart far from me, and their fear toward me is taught by the precept of men: Therefore, behold, I will proceed to do a marvellous work among this people, even a marvellous work and a wonder: for the wisdom of their wise men shall perish, and the understanding of their prudent men shall be hid.

Jeremiah 51:37-40 And Babylon shall become heaps, a dwelling place for dragons, an astonishment, and an hissing, without an inhabitant. They shall roar together like lions: they

shall yell as lions' whelps. In their heat I will make their feasts, and I will make them drunken,
that they may rejoice, and sleep a perpetual sleep, and not wake, saith the Lord. I will bring
them down like lambs to the slaughter, like rams with he goats.

Read the above and be aware! In one sense I strongly agree with some of the
spokesmen for this movement, who say that we have entered into a new epoch of
the spirit, a kind of fullness of time, or a "kairos." But the time that has come full, is
the time of judgement, the time spoken of in II Thess 2! Now is not the time for
drunkenness nor reckless abandon—it is the time for sobriety, and for seriously
critical thinking. This is the time for all Christians to decide the absolute basis of our
faith. Is it to be the faith once and for all delivered to the saints through the Holy
Scriptures? Or, is it the ongoing revelation, the faith of subjective experiences, a
kind of evolution of the church where she gets stronger and more Christlike until
she "evolves" into the "new man," the man child who will rule the nations? I believe
in the cross, the Bible, the power of the Spirit, subjective experiences with God,
casting out devils, healing, all of it! But every subjective experience in God has to be
interpreted through the objective revelation God gave us of Himself, in the holy
scriptures, once and for all delivered to the saints!

The idea that many people are going to be shocked and amazed on judgement
day, is the furthest thing from a lot of Charismatic minds. The Gospel tells us that
one day people who cast out devils and prophesied, and did other "wonderful
works" are going to be rejected! Why? *Depart from me you workers of iniquity*
[lawlessness]. *I never knew you* [approved you]. In other words, "Your did your own
thing! You pursued with zeal, what you thought was good, your idea of the 'power
of God.'" You know, "Let's use the name of Jesus to cast the devil out of whole
cities!" Would that be good? You bet! But is that a Biblical concept? Did Jesus or the
apostles do it? Or, how about, "This guy's a prophet of the Lord, he speaks with
authority, 70% of the time he's accurate." Do these modern day "prophets" mean
good or evil? I think they mean good! That one who prophesied that on Thursday,
June 9th "all evil will be ripped off the earth," wouldn't that be good? Of course!
But is it Biblical? No way! How about when Rodney Howard Browne touches some
rebellious man or woman or teen and they fall to the ground laughing and come up
in a swoon, "loving Jesus," "passionate for Jesus." Isn't that good? You see, there you
have it. "Lord, didn't we cast out devils and make war in the heavenlies? Didn't we
prophesy? Didn't we do many wonderful works," "Sure you did, but not on my
terms!" Therefore, beware, Christians won't be seduced by overt evil, the
Deception will be in the area of the good. God's good as opposed to Christianized,
humanistic, man centered, mystical good, like what's happening in Toronto. These
are no doubt good people, all of them. But where are they coming from? Why do
they think this is revival? To answer these questions, let's go back about 40-50 years
and put everything in the proper context.

End Notes

1. Richard Ostling. "Laughing for the Lord." Time Magazine. Aug 15, 1994.

2. Geoffrey Levy. "This man has been given the Toronto Blessing. What in God's name is going on?" Daily Mail. Sept 2, 1994.

3. Ibid.

4. Doucet, Daina. "Renewal Excites Canadian Churches." Charisma. June, 1994.

5. Dave Roberts. "Rumours of Revival." Alpha Magazine. July, 1994.

6. Ibid.

7. Eleanor Mumford. "Spreading Like Wildfire." Renewal. July, 1994.

8. The same article (7) goes on to quote Mark Elsdon Dew from Holy Trinity Brompton, 'The Holy Spirit has come with such power upon prayer meetings, church services, and even staff business meetings that the world "Revival" is upon everyone's lips…The Sunday services during the last two weeks have resulted in scores of bodies lying all over the floor. Those affected described how they have a renewed sense of God's love for them, a new joy and fresh vigour to serve him. This is happening at churches all over London.' Ibid.

9. Other secular headlines "Congregation Rolling in the Aisle," "Evangelical Congregation Shows Signs of the Spirit," and "Faithful Fall for the Power of the Spirit," by Fred Langan and Paul Goodman, which says, 'People from all over the world are flocking to this unlikely church the Toronto Airport branch of the Vineyard Christian Fellowship, six nights a week. And every night there are astounding scenes of people shaking with laughter, slipping into a trance, falling to the floor and crying. "Last week, Bishop David Pytches from England was down here roaring on the floor like a lion," says John Arnott, the church's pastor.'

10. Daina Doucet.

11. Ibid.

12. Ibid.

13. Bill Jackson. "What in the World is Happening to Us." Champaign Vineyard Church, Champaign, Illinois.

14. Ibid.

15. "Toronto June 94 Thoughts."

16. Daina Doucet.

17. Ibid.

18. Terry Virgo. "Fresh Outpourings of the Holy Spirit." Renewal. August, 1994.

19. Wes Campbell. "Prophet Sharing." New Life Vineyard Fellowship. 1992.

20. "Toronto June 94 Thoughts"

21. Mike Bickle and Michael Sullivant. "God's Manifest Presence, Understanding the Phenomena that Accompany the Spirit's Ministry."

22. Ibid.

23. Bill Jackson. Page 17.

24. Ibid. Page 17.

25. Ibid. Page 6.

3
A Brief, Recent History of the Progression of Pentecostal Error

Shifting Hope

We can start by looking at hope. What is it and how does it affect us? Hope is our favourable expectation, what we have to look forward to. What you hope for determines how you will live, relate to others and receive from the Lord. Though we all may have several hopes of differing degrees of intensity, everyone's life has an ultimate, overriding, expectation, either a hope or a dread. What is your ultimate (bottom line) hope? What is the Hope of the church? This is a very significant question, and worthy of our attention. It will determine much of the character and effectiveness of the church. What is it that we are to look forward to?

Traditionally, the Pentecostals and Evangelicals have hoped in the bodily return of our Lord Jesus Christ, to "rescue us from the evils of this present world." We looked forward to the "gathering together" unto Him, and the Rapture of the church, to be with the Lord in the air. We realized that any day could be the last day of possible impact for us on this earth. Consequently, the Pentecostal Movement has had one of the greatest missionary thrusts of any movement ever. The heavenly minded, contrary to popular opinion, have always done the most earthly good! The Pentecostal Hymnody has been an example of this hope. Songs like, "I'll Fly Away," "Changed in the Twinkling of an Eye," "Victory in Jesus," "When We All Get to Heaven," "We Shall See the King," and "I'm Getting Ready to Leave This World," have helped to both reflect and nurture this cherished hope. We have been pilgrims, passing through this world.

But our hope has shifted, and this shift has brought consequences. As one California pastor with a nationally known ministry has said,

> I used to sing all those unscriptural songs..."This world is not my home, I'm just passing through; My treasures are laid up away beyond the blue..." Did you ever sing that one? I've got news for you. This world is your home. Forever, according to the Word [of God]...Our final home is right here on earth.[1]

We have shifted from a God centered heavenly expectation to a man centered, "We [the church] must conquer for Christ" before Jesus comes back. The hope has shifted from expecting God to complete our redemption and judge the world in righteousness, to the church rising up in "power and glory" and doing exploits!

Triumphalism

The above mentioned shift in hope, began as a trickle in Evangelical and Pentecostal circles, but has been steadily gaining momentum, to the point where triumphalism in one form or another is now the predominant view in the church. To people who hold to this view, the idea of a "Rapture" is an evasion of our responsibilities, a "defeatist," helicopter escape theory, (the idea of being rescued from heaven, somehow unworthy of overcomers).

There are two major forms of triumphalism that have captured the popular Christian imagination at this time. The Evangelical form is the "We've got to take back our country from the humanists" variety. We are "taking dominion" over every aspect of our culture and ruling and reigning for Christ. Art, politics, education, communication, all are "ground that needs to be taken" for Christ, and controlled by Christians. Allegedly, we are the leaven, which ultimately effects the whole lump (society) for Christ! This belief has been confusing Gen 1:26 with Matt 28:18-20, telling Christians we have a "dominion mandate" to exercise over society.

This movement has touched Pentecostals, but its primary appeal is to the non-Charismatic oriented Evangelical. Authors like Gary North, Gary Demar, David Chilton, and others have brilliantly set forth both their doctrine and agenda for the reconstruction of society. This movement received great impetus in the 1980s, both with the political dissatisfaction of American Christians, as well as, the failure of Jesus to return by 1988 as many Christians expected. (Popular prophecy teachers had interpreted Matt 24 to teach that within 40 years of the establishment of national Israel [May, 1948], Jesus would return, 40 years being a generation). The Reconstruction movement and its wider implications have been well documented and discussed in Dave Hunt's excellent book, **Whatever Happened To Heaven?**

Pentecostal Triumphalism

There is another side of triumphalism however, a supernatural as opposed to political/cultural dominionism. For at least 40 years, but undoubtedly longer, there has been an alternative hope fostered in Pentecostal circles. It is the hope of a "Great End Times Revival," which would "shake the whole world," and bring whole nations to Jesus! The church won't be a "whipped, sick, defeated little group huddled in the corner, hiding from the Antichrist," but rather, a might army, ruling the nations, displaying raw power, emptying hospitals, filling stadiums, the awe of the whole world! All of this takes place, allegedly, **before** the return of our Lord. The question of Luke 18 is almost irrelevant, in this view. *Will the son of man find faith when He comes to earth?* Of course, He will, more faith than ever!!! A man centered hope has replaced for us the old hope of the church.

Titus 2:13 Looking for the blessed hope, and the glorious appearing of the great God and our Saviour Jesus Christ.

I believe that it is only in this context that you can ever begin to understand what is happening in Toronto and other places all over the world. Please allow me to take you back about 40 some years.

The Evangelical Awakening of the Late 40s

All kinds of good things were bursting forth from the kingdom of God, in the post World War II years. It seemed as though God was blowing aside the strife and death lingering over the globe, with a fresh breeze of His Spirit. Between the years of 1946-1956, there was simultaneously an Evangelical Awakening as well as a Pentecostal Healing and Deliverance Revival. On college campuses all over the country in the late 40s and early 50s spontaneous, sovereign revivals sprung forth. God was doing "terrible things, which we weren't looking for." Just two random examples, Wheaton College in Illinois and Asbury Seminary in Kentucky, in February 1950, both had revivals, which were reported on in **Life Magazine, Time,** and numerous other national news sources! It was in 1948 that Billy Graham gained national prominence as an evangelist, Bill Bright began campus work in those days, Fuller, his seminary in 1947, World Vision started in the early 1950s.

Internationally the times were marked by an unusual degree of God's graciousness. Astounding revivals broke out in the British and Scottish Isles, particularly in the Isle of Lewis and Harris in 1949, also known as the Hebrides Isles. To give you a taste of the evangelical awakening, here is an eyewitness account of the Hebrides Revival of 1949.

> The service closed in a tense silence and the building emptied. As he came down from the pulpit, a young deacon raised his hand moving it in a circle above his head, whispered, "Mr. Campbell, God is hovering over. He is going to break through. I can hear the rumbling of heaven's chariot wheels." Just then the door opened and an elder beckoned, "Come and see what's happening!" The entire congregation was lingering outside, reluctant to disperse, others had joined them, drawn from their homes by an irresistible power they had not experienced before. There were looks of deep distress on many faces. Suddenly, a cry pierced the silence. A young man who had remained in the church, burdened to the point of agony for his fellow man, was pouring out his desire in prayer. He was so overcome that he fell into a trance and as he lay prostrate on the floor, the congregation swept back into the church. The awful presence of God brought a wave of conviction of sin that caused even mature Christians to feel their sinfulness, bringing groans of distress and prayers of repentance from the unconverted. Strong men bowed under the weight of sin and cries for mercy were mingled with shouts of joy from others who had passed into life.

Now that is revival! Based on the preaching of the Word, attended with "solemn conviction," initiated by the sovereign God, bringing repentance! Glory to God!

The Pentecostal Revival of the 1940s - 1950s

The post World War II years were a tremendous time of awakening for the Pentecostals as well. It was during those years that God graciously granted a tremendous visitation of healing and gifts of the Spirit, according to His will. These were the days when men like Oral Roberts, Jack Coe, David Nunn, A. A. Allen, and T. L. Osborne were launched into powerful healing ministries that absolutely astounded the multitudes. Reading the accounts of T. L. Osborne in his chapter, "The Results," from his book, **Healing the Sick**, is like reading the Book of Acts on an even larger scale! Here are some excerpts,

> February 9, 1949: Kingston, Jamaica, one deaf mute was healed. Two blind were healed, they could see my hand and count my fingers. Many stroke victims and lame and sick folks were healed...As I left the auditorium, I met a blind woman in the street. She heard my voice and begged me to pray for her. I did and she was completely and instantly healed! She could count my fingers out in the dark, could see the stars in the heavens and walked away in the night unaided, praising God...[2]

You get stories of this kind, over and over again and not just in the Third World countries, but everywhere in the world. I have no doubt that these things happened. Healing is completely scriptural. We can expect "signs and wonders to follow those who believe." God is ever gracious and it pleases Him to reveal His healing mercy to the world.

The effect of the great healing ministries began to wane toward the late 1950s and to many, the healing ministry came into disrepute. Of course, divine healing itself is scriptural and above reproach no matter what anyone says. However it is in the vessels of mercy that there are problems at times. All that our loving Father has chosen to work with is men, sinners. Just because a man has been gifted by God, it doesn't mean that he will always exhibit the character of Christ, or even remain true to Jesus. As it is written, *The gifts and callings of God are without repentance.* Like Samson, there have been a few notorious examples of healing evangelists falling prey to their own desires.

Three Messages of the Healing Movement

I believe that the primary aspect of every movement has to be, not the manifestation, but the message that it presents. The healing revival brought three major messages to the body. Supremely, was the message of the importance of unity in the body of Christ. They often preached that, "for this cause many are weak and sickly and die early," because they failed to rightly discern the mystical body of Christ. In those gigantic tent meetings, God showed people that he is no respecter of persons, nor denominations. Baptists, Presbyterians, Methodists, and even Catholics (gasp!) as well as some Pentecostals were healed by the hand of the Lord. The healing ministries saw in this a day coming when the denominational system would give way to "one body in Christ." This message has remained a supreme aspiration for many to this day, and the desire for unity at almost any cost is at a zenith!

Another message that was stressed was the restoration concept. The idea was that since the days of the early church, various truths of Christian experience have been lost. But even as Luther was used to restore justification by faith, Wesley, the sanctification message, the Baptists, the return of Christ, even the Pentecostals were used to restore the baptism of the Holy Ghost and divine healing. The anticipation developed that, before Jesus returns there would be a complete restoration of New Testament Christianity, including restoration of apostles, prophets, pastors, teachers, and evangelists. This doctrine has subsequently taken on a life of its own and produced a variety of errant views, of which much of today's error springs from. I think that the premise is wrong. Who says that the true church lost any truths that need to be restored?

The third message stressed is that these are indeed the final days before the return of Jesus Christ. "Get ready everyone, Jesus is coming, and these healings are a sign to you of this fact!" To which I say, Amen!

A Deuteronomy ch13 Test

In those days also, a simple, obscure man rose to prominence in healing ministry. Eventually, he came to be regarded as a prophet of God. His name was William Branham. His unique life marked a turning point for American Pentecostalism. He did represent a test from God. (Deut 13:1-5) The kind of test in which we, in failing, have to a degree lost our eyesight (discernment). This will become more clear as we look at his interesting and unusual life.

William Branham was born 100 years and 10 miles from the time and place that Abe Lincoln was born, deep in the hills of Kentucky. He was born to very simple and poor parents. His mother was only 15 and his father was 18 years old. It has been reported that when visitors and well wishers came to the log shack to see the child, they also saw an otherworldly light resting over the babe.

Branham, who was the first of ten children, reports of his early life that, "There was always a peculiar feeling, like someone standing near me, trying to say something to me, and especially when I was alone." In fact, when he was seven years old, he had a strange visitation.

I was on my way one afternoon to carry water to the house from the barn, which was about a city block away. About halfway between the house and the barn stood an old poplar tree. I had just gotten home from school and the other boys were going out to a pond to fish. I was crying to go, but Dad said that I had to pack water. I stopped under the tree to rest when all of a sudden I heard a sound as of the wind blowing the leaves. I knew that it wasn't blowing any other place. It seemed to be a very still afternoon. I stepped back from the tree and noticed that in a certain place, about the size of a barrel, the wind seemed to be blowing through the tree leaves. Then there came a voice saying, "Never drink, smoke, or defile your body in any way for I have a work for you to do when you get older." [3]

Now this visitation made Branham afraid. It would be some time before he was converted. In his early 20s, after being healed of a life threatening condition, Branham gave his life to God. He became a Baptist preacher, held a tent meeting in Jeffersonville, Indiana, and started a church (the Branham Tabernacle.) One day he wandered into a tent meeting of Pentecostals. They asked him to preach, and recognized the call on his life. That tent meeting had a profound impact on Branham. Later he said that they had something he lacked! After excitedly telling his wife, her family and his friends of the experience, people talked him out of mingling with "those folks," so he backed away. In 1937, while he was both pastoring and working as a game warden, the Ohio River flooded, killing both his wife and young baby. Branham believed that it was a judgement from God for his refusal to join the Pentecostals. Shortly after that, he joined the United Pentecostal Churches, or the "oneness" people (Jesus only). These are people who believe that the doctrine of the trinity is "of the devil." There is an incident from this period in his life that underscores the unusual quality of it. He was preparing to baptize 130 people in the Ohio River. According to Gordon Lindsey:

As Brother Branham was about to baptize the 17th person, he heard a still small voice which said, "Look up." Three times the words were repeated. He looked up and there from the sky appeared a bright star. After a few seconds had passed, the people looked up and many of the people saw the star also. Some fainted, others shouted, and still others ran away. Then the star apparently was withdrawn back into the sky. The incident created such an interest that an account of it appeared in the local newspaper. [4]

Branham's whole life was marked by strange episodes like this. More than once, people reported either seeing a halo, or his head bathed in a strange, intense light! I have in my files two copies of photographs taken which capture this phenomena. One photograph was taken by a man hired by one of Branham's detractors. When the photo was developed, a halo appeared above Branham's head! That's right, a halo! The photographer was so impressed that he immediately took the photo to the hotel where Branham was staying. The Branham people had the photo examined by a professional investigator of questionable documents. He signed an affidavit attesting to the fact that the photo had not been tampered with. How do you question a man with a halo?

One of the strangest experiences happened in May of 1946. Branham was still an obscure pastor, working also as a game warden to make ends meet. On that day, he relates, "While walking...under a maple tree, it seemed that the whole top of the tree let loose. It seemed that something came down through the tree like a great, rushing, wind...”[5] His wife heard the sound and came rushing out of the house to ask the badly shaken Branham what was happening. He realized that it was his crisis time, finally, the time had come to find out his life's calling and to confront "the presence" which had followed him through his life. Branham went off to a cabin in the woods to pray, (in his own words).

> Then along in the night, at about the 11th hour, I had quit praying and was sitting up when I noticed a light flickering in the room. Thinking someone was coming with a flashlight I looked out of the window, but there was no one, and when I looked back the light was spreading out on the floor, becoming wider...As the light was spreading...I became excited...as I looked up, there hung that great star...looked like a ball of fire or light shining down on the floor...coming through the light I saw the feet of a man coming towards me, as naturally as you could walk towards me. He appeared to be a man who...clothed in a white robe, he had a smooth face, no beard, dark hair down to his shoulders, rather dark complexioned, with a very pleasant countenance...Seeing how fearful I was, he began to speak, "Fear not, I am sent from the presence of Almighty God to tell you that your peculiar life and your misunderstood ways have been to indicate that God has sent you to take a gift of divine healing to the peoples of the world. If you will be sincere and can get the people to believe you, nothing shall stand before your prayer, not even cancer."[6]

The angel went on to tell Branham that he would have two sign gifts, the ability to tell people the secrets of their hearts and past life and the ability to detect diseases by the vibrations of his left hand. This visitation would mark a turning point for his ministry. It was shortly after this that Branham was catapulted to national prominence.

Signs and Wonders

Branham's ministry was nothing short of amazing. I have seen video tapes of Branham. One was a particular Full Gospel Businessmen's Fellowship meeting in the mid 1950s. Branham and the crowd were obviously waiting for the sign gift ministry to begin. "You know what I'm waiting for, the angel of the Lord, I can't start without him." Gradually, he would say something like, "Now he's here," and the sign gift ministry would start. He would calmly call individuals out of the crowd, tell them the secrets of their heart, the diseases of their body, what the doctor said, what they said to their wife the previous night, and then calmly pronounce them healed. Often they were! Not always then?!

People who knew Branham are all agreed on at least two points. One, his genuine character of humility and compassion. Branham lacked hype or any showmanship at all. The other thing all agreed upon was his absolute accuracy, in words of knowledge and wisdom. The late Ern Baxter (commonly known as one of the Fort Lauderdale Five, shepherding leaders of the 1970s) was a teacher travelling with Branham for some years. Baxter has made the comment that he never heard Branham give an inaccurate word of knowledge to any person. And Branham ministered to tens of thousands, perhaps hundreds of thousands! F.F. Bosworth, a pioneer healing evangelist and author of **Christ, the Healer** said of Branham,

> At these times, he can say with absolute certainty, "Thus saith the Lord," and he is never wrong. He told me last week he simply acts out what he already has seen himself doing in a vision. The success phase of his ministry is exactly 100%.[7]

I could go on and on about Branham, for truly his life and ministry were astounding. Calmly and deliberately, he would affect incredible healings and deliverances. Over and over again he would tell people what their name, address, conversation, troubles, diseases, sometimes sins, friends, etc., by the Spirit, with complete accuracy! There were also incredibly dramatic showdowns with crazed lunatics, who would be allowed to get to Branham, spewing out blasphemies and threatenings and yet be unable to actually do anything except either shirk away or repent, all in front of huge audiences. Pentecostals have never seen anything like it before or since! To this day, the Pentecostal media hold him up in a reverent light. He died on Christmas Eve, 1965, at the age of 56, in a car accident. His followers wouldn't allow him to be buried, believing that he would be raised from the dead on Easter, 1966! Eventually and reluctantly, he was buried.

One "Small" Detail

Have you noticed one detail in this brief biography I have left out? Think about it. I told you of the signs, wonders, humility, character, accuracy, and renown. However, one aspect is saved for last. His teaching.

Deut. 13:1-5 If there arise among you a prophet, or a dreamer of dreams, and giveth thee a sign or a wonder, and the sign or the wonder come to pass, whereof he spake unto thee, saying, Let us go after other gods, which thou hast not known, and let us serve them; Thou shalt not hearken unto the words of that prophet, or that dreamer of dreams; for the Lord your God proveth you, to know whether ye love the Lord your God with all your heart and with all your soul. Ye shall walk after the Lord your God, and fear him, and keep his commandments, and obey his voice, and ye shall serve him, and cleave unto him. And that prophet, or that dreamer of dreams, shall be put to death; because he hath spoken to turn you away from the Lord your God, which brought you out of the land of Egypt, and redeemed you out of the house of bondage, to thrust thee out of the way which the Lord thy God commanded thee to walk in. So shalt thou put the evil away from the midst of thee.

Now is the time for us to re-examine both Deut 18 and Deut 13. The teaching is that if anyone calls himself a prophet and is inaccurate at all, speaking in the name of the Lord, you are not to fear him (Deut 18). But Deut 13 tells us that a prophet can arise, who is accurate in his gifts, but still is a false prophet. Why is this? Because God can allow the accuracy to test the loyalty of His people. The question is, will we live by bread alone? Or by every word that comes from God? Will we be dazzled by powerful signs and wonders? Or do we loyally uphold **the truth** of God? If false prophets can have accurate gifts, and people get healed and predictions come to pass, how can you tell if they are true or false? By examining the **content** of their teaching. This is the test we keep failing. We get so intoxicated by signs, wonders, prophecies, words, healings, crowds, and personality, that we overlook doctrinal error. After all, we don't argue over "doctrinal gnats," do we?

Branham's Teaching

What did he teach? For that matter, what does Paul Cain, Mike Bickle, Bob Jones, John Wimber, Bill Hammon, Roger Forster, Gerald Coates, or anyone else who is part of the "prophetic move" teach? For the teaching is much more significant than the manifestation. The teaching is one of the fruits you can "know them by."

Branham believed that we are in what he called, "God's seventh church age," based on the letters to the church in Revelation. According to Branham, "the angels of the churches," were different men down through church history, who brought the church along, through new revelation. In fact, his tombstone, in Jeffersonville, Indiana, is shaped like a pyramid. On one side are the names of the seven churches. On the other side are the names of the messengers to each church, Paul, Irenaeus, Martin, Columba, Luther, Wesley, and of course, Branham.

The impact of the United Pentecostal Church is evident in his teaching. Branham also believed that the doctrine of the trinity was Babylonian and even "of the devil."[8] To him, the Father, Son and Holy Spirit, are three different "attributes" of Jesus.

Stranger yet, Branham taught that the Word of God was given in three forms, the zodiac, the Egyptian pyramids, and the written scripture.[9] Another strange doctrine, was his teaching on the "serpent's seed," the idea that Eve had sexual relations with Satan and produced the line of Cain, an evil "seed" which is continually being propagated to this day. The effect of this doctrine has a tendency towards misogyny, making women responsible for keeping the "seed" alive.

It is my conviction that the Pentecostal movement stood at a crossroads in regards to Branham—would we judge the heresy in loyalty to the truth of the gospel? Or, would we look at it in a pragmatic way and say, "Look at the crowds! He brings people to God! How could this be of Satan? Would Satan heal? We've been begging God for signs and wonders, they're here! His critics are nothing, they don't "produce the goods," they're probably not even spirit filled, no anointing, just criticism." Though there were no doubt many voices raised against Branham's heresies, by and large, Branham enjoyed great acceptance by the truly influential leaders of Pentecostalism. (To this day, he is regarded by many as a prophet and pioneer of the signs and wonders movement.) It is true that at the time of his death, his popularity was waning and his teaching became more obvious, but to the Manifested Sons of God Movement, as well as much of Christian media, and even the current "miracle ministries" and Charismatic leaders, there is a profound respect for him and in many cases a desire to emulate him. As Al Dager says, "To date, William Branham's body is still in the grave. But his occult methodology of healing was picked up by hundreds of pastors and teachers upon whom he had laid his hands and who have traded on it to a greater or lesser degree."[10]

End Notes

1. Gary Greenwald. "End Time Eschatology: The Rapture Rip Off" Sermon preached at Eagles Nest. February 4, 1987.
2. T.L. Osborne. Healing the Sick. Harrison.
3. Gordon Lindsey. William Branham: A Man Sent From God. Page 30-31.
4. Ibid. Page 71.
5. Ibid. Page 76.
6. Ibid. Page 77.
7. Ibid. Page 172-173.
8. Al Dager. Vengeance is Ours. Sword. Page 55.
9. Al Dager. Vengeance is Ours. Sword. Page 59.

4
The Latter Rain and Manifested Sons of God

A New Thing

The visibility and popularity of the healing revivalists, especially William Branham, had seemingly renewed the Pentecostal Movement. What was God doing? What would He do next? At certain times a particular passage of scripture will grip the church as a whole (II Chronicles 7:14 seemed to be on everyone's mind during the mid to late 1980s). In the late 1940s for Pentecostals the verse was found in Isa 43:18-19. An incredible expectation was developing that God was going to do a "new thing."

Isaiah 43:18-19 Remember ye not the former things, neither consider the things of old. Behold, I will do a new thing; now it shall spring forth; shall ye not know it? I will even make a way in the wilderness, and rivers in the desert.

George Hawtin, a Pentecostal pastor and director of an orphanage and Bible school, attended a William Branham meeting in Vancouver, British Columbia, in 1947. He was the head of the ministry called "the Sharon Work," in North Battleford, Saskatchewan. He with several students and faculty members, had attended the Branham meeting and they even received an "impartation" from Branham, through laying on of hands. Hawtin wrote a glowing report on the meeting in the January 1, 1948 edition of the **Sharon Star,**

...In Vancouver...the deaf received their hearing. I heard the dumb speak...I saw a goitre vanish. I saw sick people get up from their beds...to my best knowledge, I did not see one person who was not healed when Brother Branham took time to pray specially for him. I came home from these meetings realizing as never before that the real gifts of the Holy Spirit are far mightier than anything we have imagined in our wildest dreams...All great outpourings of the past have had their outstanding truths. Luther's truth was justification by faith; Wesley's was sanctification; the Baptists taught the pre-millennial coming of Christ; the Missionary Alliance taught divine healing; the Pentecostal outpouring has restored the baptism of the Holy Spirit to its rightful place. But the next great outpouring is going to be marked by all these other truths, plus such a demonstration of the nine gifts of the Spirit as the world, not even the apostolic world, has ever witnessed before.[1]

People like Branham had whetted the appetite of the church for signs, wonders, and New Testament Christianity. A book came out at the same time (1946) that enjoyed widespread popularity among Pentecostals and contributed to the general expectation of a "new day." It was called, **Atomic Power with God, Through**

Fasting and Prayer,[2] by Franklin Hall. This peculiar book taught that those who would learn to control their appetites could come into a supernatural, and miracle lifestyle. Hawtin commented that this book had an effect on the Sharon Brethren. To those "who could receive it," answered prayer, signs, wonders, immortality, and even release from gravity awaited those who would fast and pray. This is indeed a strange book, but as Al Dager points out in **Vengeance Is Ours**, this book was publicly acknowledged as having a major influence on many of the Faith Healers of the day.

The New Thing Springs Forth

It was into this time and atmosphere of expectation that a visitation occurred, at the Sharon Work in North Battleford. **Vengeance is Ours** explains this occurrence:

> On February 11, 1948, a young woman at the Bible school prophesied that a great revival was about to break out. The next day, according to George Hawtin, the Holy Spirit fell with great power. [Quoting Hawtin] "Day after day the glory and power of God came among us. Great repentance, humbling, fasting, and prayer prevailed in everyone." News of the events at North Battleford spread and soon people were coming from everywhere in hope of receiving spiritual power.[3]

By July, 1948, the Sharon Brethren put on a huge camp meeting which attracted several thousand from the United States, Canada, and all over the world, all wanting to be part of the "New Thing!" In a short time, the Latter Rain Movement was a worldwide phenomena.

What Do You Mean, Latter Rain?

James 5:7 Be patient therefore, brethren, unto the coming of the Lord. Behold, the husbandman waiteth for the precious fruit of the earth, and hath long patience for it, until he receive **the early** *and* **latter rain.**

Hosea 6:3 Then shall we know, if we follow on to know the Lord: his going forth is prepared as the morning; and he shall come unto us as the rain, as **the latter** *and* **former rain** *unto the earth.*

Joel 2:23 Be glad then, ye children of Zion and rejoice in the Lord your God; for he hath given you the former rain moderately, and he will cause to come down for you the rain, **the former rain,** *and the* **latter rain** *in the first month.*

In both the Old and the New Testament, there is an allegory used for God's blessing, based on the cycle of rains in the Holy Land. The "former rain" is crucial for planting, it is a type of the giving of the Law on Sinai, on the day of Pentecost. The "latter rain" is a reference to the outpouring of the Spirit in Acts 2, also on Pentecost. Peter interpreted it so when he said, "This is that spoken of by Joel the prophet." The former rain, the law, is for softening the ground for planting. In other words, the Law of Moses, and the Ten Commandments can be used to bring conviction to the hard hearted. The "latter rain" is essential for the actual harvest, in other words, the baptism of the Holy Spirit which God poured out on Pentecost, is vital to make us witnesses and the New Testament time is harvest time, as it is written, "now is the day of salvation." All of this is quite simple and obvious. In the Holy Land, the harvest rains are more intense than the early rains, as they are essential in maturing the crop for harvest, and as we know the New Testament is greater than the Old, we have a superior covenant based on a better promise.

But there is a different, recent interpretation to this allegory. "Latter Rain" people believe that the lesser, former rains, are represented by Acts 2, Pentecost. Therefore, we still have the great "latter rain" outpouring to look forward to. The Spirit will supposedly be poured out so strong, in these last days, that whole nations will turn to God in one day. The important thing to note is the timing. It will not happen after Jesus returns bodily, rather before. The latter rain is therefore a radically different expectation of what the church should be looking forward to. In this view, things will only get better on earth, until the Second Coming.

Restoration

A major tenet of the "Latter Rain" teaching is the Restoration concept. According to this erroneous view, down through the centuries the church "lost" different concepts and experiences in the Lord, i.e. justification by faith, sanctification, divine healing, speaking in tongues, and apostolic ministry. So, gradually, God has had to restore these truths. Martin Luther was supposedly used to restore justification by faith, Wesley, sanctification, people such as Dowie, divine healing, the Azuza Street Revival restored the baptism of the Holy Spirit, and etc. The Latter Rain believes that the work of restoration is not over yet. They hold that Davidic worship, teaching, ministry, evangelists, and prophets and even apostles in all of their authority are currently being restored. According to a commonly held misunderstanding of Acts 3:21, they teach that Jesus can't come back even though He wants to because **WE** haven't fully "restored all things."

Thus, the "Latter Rain" Revival centered around the following themes: Restoration of fivefold ministry (Eph 4) (especially apostles and prophets.) This teaching is crucial because it is this ministry that is supposedly going to unite the church, and perfect the Body of Christ; the restoration of personal prophecy, the impartation of spiritual gifts through laying on of hands; deliverance, healing and baptism of the Spirit through laying on of hands, and the complete unity of the Body of Christ. Denominationalism was seen as "Babylonian Captivity" and subsequently a host of churches affected by the "Latter Rain" broke away from their denominations and became independent churches, many being "set into the body" by the newly discovered apostles. This "revival" which started in Canada, was primarily about Christians "coming into their own fullness," and not necessarily the conversion of sinners.

Obviously, you can tell I don't believe in the "restoration" model of the church. How could the church lose justification? Justification by faith is the whole basis for the church, the church has always had it as well as sanctification, healing and the baptism of the Holy Spirit. There has always been the true church which has been equipped by Jesus Himself, the Shepherd and Bishop of our souls. What Luther, Wesley, and the others did is what all true Christians have done down through time. They took what God gave them and introduced others to it. But they couldn't have "restored" it to the church. The church has always been complete in Christ! If you buy the restoration concept, it inevitably sets you up for the evolutionary church concept, a deluding, intoxicating idea that makes the current expression of the church feel that she is the **ultimate** center of God's purposes, over and above all previous expressions of the church. Let's not flatter ourselves.

The Evolutionary Church Model

If Restoration and Latter Rain are true scriptural teaching, then we are more anointed, better equipped and more powerful than any other church in history. As Earl Paulk has said,

> The last enemy to be conquered is death. Who will conquer it? A mature church will come forth, with the kind of authority and power that will be able to stand in the very face of Satan. When the church reaches that level of maturity, God will be able to say, "This generation of the church does not need to die. She has reached a place of maturity. I will translate her because her maturity pleases me."[4]

Here is a classic example of what I call the Evolution Church Model. As if to say, "at last, after 2000 years, the church has matured enough to please God." The church is the family of God, which is in heaven and on earth at the same time. She is not, nor has ever had to "progress in maturity." She has always been "complete in Christ" and yet on an individual basis, the members of the body have always been at various stages of personal maturity. If you hear a statement like, "In the Book of Acts, we have the church in her infancy," you are hearing a form of evolution. Paulk would have us believe that no other church has arrived at the level we have attained to. According to Galatians, the Old Testament of Law was infancy and childhood. But the New Testament faith is mature manhood. The true church has always been complete!

The evolution concept of the church fosters pride and arrogance. Both Rick Joyner and Mike Bickle have said, in effect, that the apostles of the Book of Acts will want to wait in line to interview the superapostles of our day.

An interesting example of the evolutionary model of the church is a little book written in 1951 by George Warnock called **The Feast of Tabernacles**. This book is a virtual primer of Latter Rain, Manifested Sons of God teaching, which still enjoys a wide circulation today. According to Warnock, the feasts of Israel described in

Leviticus 23, are a pattern for the progress of the church through time. Starting at Passover, which is Calvary, the church has been passing through the different feasts, over the years, to Pentecost. Warnock writes that we, the church, still have to go through the Day of Atonement, the Feast of Trumpets, and come into the Feast of Tabernacles, which to him represents God's consummate purposes for us, the Last Days Church. When we come into Tabernacles, which was a tremendous time of celebration for Israel, God will finally dwell within His people. I have heard many people take Warnock's ideas and interpret the present, mystical revival as the fulfilment of the Feast of Tabernacles.

The Manifested Sons of God

In 1948, the Assemblies of God confronted and denounced the extremes of the Latter Rain Movement, and teachers among them fell into disrepute. Not many would want to openly admit to being of the Latter Rain or its offshoot, the Manifested Sons. In fact, people balk at those labels to this day. However, the doctrines and concepts of this heresy have continued to be promoted, frequently recurring under different names, but using the same premises. When a Charismatic Bible teacher, or media personality prophesies of that "great end time army," that will "take nations for God," and "usher in the kingdom of God!" or give birth to the "next revival," call him a Manifested Sons teacher and see what he does. Usually they balk, because of the scandal and some of the extremes associated with those titles, but in effect, that is what they are espousing!

What do we mean when we say Manifested Sons of God? We mean those people who took the Latter Rain doctrine a little further in its logical progression. The label comes from Romans 8:19.

Romans 8:19 *For the earnest expectation of the creature waiteth for the manifestation of the sons of God.*

Manifested Sons of God teaching, in a nutshell, is "since all creation is waiting for the Manifested Sons of God to appear, so it (creation) can be delivered from corruption, what are we waiting for? Let's hurry up and realize that we, corporately, are the Christ and the sooner we realize that, the sooner we can mature into our full stature and be all that God intended us to be. We can crush God's enemies, even death, and usher in the kingdom of God and take the world for Jesus through the miracle working power that is within us. Boy, have we been dense! We have been waiting for God to save us from this world in that "helicopter escape," the Rapture, when all of this time, He has been waiting for us to get it together. We must realize who we really are in Christ, and the power within us and rise up and do what the church down through time has either been too carnal or too immature to ever do. The church must now put all of God's enemies under her feet. We've been foolishly waiting for Christ to come "for us" and all the while, He's been wanting to "come within us." That, in a nutshell, is the philosophy of the Manifested Sons of God. You have all heard it in some form or another. If not called Latter Rain, it's come to you in the shepherding movement. There are many different Charismatic strains of it including Word Faith, Kingdom Now, Dominion, The Prophetic Move, and of course, this laughing "revival." As Bill Hamon says,

> The earth and all of creation is waiting for the manifestation of the sons of God, the time when they will come into their maturity and immortalization...The church has a responsibility and ministry to the rest of creation. Earth and its natural creation is anxiously waiting for the church to reach full maturity and come to full sonship. When the church realizes its full sonship, its bodily redemption will cause a redemptive chain reaction throughout all creation.[5]

The error is in the focus. This focus has been shifted from Christ as the ultimate consummation of God's purposes, to us, the church. We won't ever come into enough perfection or spiritual maturity, in and of ourselves, to become immortal. Christ is the One who will change us at His appearing, in a moment, in the twinkling of an eye, at His coming. Only then will this "corruptible put on incorruption" and death will be swallowed up in victory. Christ does it alone in His glory, not us! Romans 8:19 refers to the time after the second coming of Christ, the resurrection, when our salvation will be completed and our bodies changed. All creation waits for that day, on that day, the curse of futility will be removed from the earth and all creation will be free! The difference between orthodox theology and Manifested Sons of God thought is in the focus. Orthodoxy is Christ centered, and Manifested Sons of God is man centered.

Do They Believe That the Entire Church Will Be Immortal?

As Manifested Sons of God theology developed, it became obvious that not all of the church would "buy into" the immortalization of the believer, a la pre-second coming. In fact, the vast majority of the church will be too carnal and insensitive to receive "the revelation." As Bill Britton, an early Manifested Sons of God teacher says,

> Although there will be unnumbered multitudes of people saved by the Grace of God, through the precious blood of Jesus...The real purposes of God are tied up in that group of saints who press their way into the mark of the high calling of God...They are the 100 fold fruit of the earth, brought forth by the Latter Rain...They are the ones who put Satan under their feet and gain back the inheritance lost by Adam and much more beyond that.[6]

This elite concept of a special company of super spiritual saints, in whom "the real purposes of God are tied up in," is very appealing to people. Who would just want to be in the general number of the redeemed, when you could be "the principal wheat?" Jude says that these are they who separate themselves, talking about being either 30-60-100 fold Christians, or outer court, inner court, and of course, Holy of Holies believers. We all know that Jesus had the three, the twelve and the seventy. A spiritual elitism has developed. The same kind of thinking carries over today in the "New Breed Concept" of Mike Bickle, Paul Cain, and John Wimber.

There's apostles, there's imminent apostles and there's most imminent apostles...There's various levels of apostles and the Lord was showing us that...out of this movement would be 35 apostles...That will be the highest level of apostolic ministry...the government rests on apostles and prophets...[7]

John Wimber could see a day when,

There will be a time where even as in Acts 2, suddenly, as they were gathered, in the midst of them, the Lord came and with an anointing beyond anything that has ever been given to man before. Something astounding, so marvellous that God has kept it as a mystery as it were, behind his back, and He is about to reveal it to the ages. He is about to reveal it. With the judgement of all mankind will come this incredible incarnational enduement of God's spirit and we will see the Elijah's...This end time army will be made of the Elijah's of the Lord God...[8]

These "Elijah's," "Imminent Apostles," "Joel's Army," or whatever other name you call them, are said to have come into the revelation that they are the "corporate Christ," or the "ongoing incarnation of Christ." These are the ones who supposedly will put death under their feet, demonstrate incredible signs and wonders, bring the church in to the fullness of the stature of Christ, and submit the kingdoms of this world to become the kingdoms of our Lord and His Christ. Though this idea was officially rejected when it was first promoted in the late 1940s, it went underground, and has steadily been promoted, using different "catch phrases," until it now has become almost the dominant view. Let's look at a few of its troubling particulars, and proponents.

Manifested Sons of God Promotes Distorted Christology
The whole premise for a book written by Bill Britton called **Jesus, the Pattern Son**, can be summed up in this sentence from its preface.

The life of Jesus in His humanity here on earth was a divine pattern for the perfect, end time body of Christ.[9]

In short, Jesus is the pattern for the ultimate expression of God: **us** of course, the **end-time** body of Christ. There is a blurring of distinction between the roles of

Christ and His church, and even the person of Christ and we, the church. It amounts to an exalting of the "new man."

> The very life of Jesus Christ is reproduced in fragile earthen vessels of this human clay...it is the perfecting into maturity of the Christ who came into our hearts as the seed when we received Him as Saviour.[10]

Is he telling us that Christ comes into us as a seed and needs to be perfected in us? This is a totally inverted concept. Christ, Himself, is complete in and of Himself, and in Him we partake of His completeness! (You may accuse me of splitting hairs, but this is a telling point!) In his teaching on the day of Atonement, George Warnock tells us that the two goats typify Christ as the head and Christ in the fullness of His people, His body. He then makes this statement, "Christ the head, therefore, is not complete without Christ, the body...Christ is the body, the whole body and not just the head."[11] Through the use of allegory, he has managed to invert a valid biblical concept! We can understand the statement, "You are not complete, except in Christ." However, Warnock and the Manifested Sons teachers reverse that statement, teaching that Christ is not complete without us! This confusion of Christ and His body is what is underscored in the whole Manifested Sons Movement right up to these times!

The Ongoing Incarnation

Do people still teach the concept of a developing and therefore incomplete Christ? Absolutely. James Robison, internationally known Bible teacher, has been quoted as saying,

> God wants us to see Jesus as merely a big brother in a huge family of brothers and sisters. You have the divine nature, the eternal life of God. God reveals that Christ had to be formed, even in Jesus.

Kenneth Hagin, a leading Faith Movement proponent has said that "The believer is just as much an incarnation as Jesus was." In this distorted view, Jesus is merely the pattern of what any "born again, spirit filled believer can be." It's ironic that Bill Britton was considered a heretic for promoting these ideas before his death. Yet, Earl Paulk openly talks about the incarnation in these terms,

> Jesus was God in the flesh. We must be as He was in the world in volume and influence.

and

> The completion of the incarnation of God in the world must be in His church...Jesus Christ is the firstfruits, but without the ongoing harvest, the incarnation will never be complete.

and amazingly,

We are on earth as extensions of God to finish the work He began. We are the essence of God, His ongoing incarnation in the world.

Now this is a gauge of the conditioning effected by this kind of doctrine. We are not talking about Bill Britton and George Warnock here, whose ideas were denounced by the Pentecostal denominations, and considered heretical. These are men who have worldwide ministries and are regularly accepted on Christian television as spiritual leaders. If Paulk's star has diminished at all, tragically it is not because of false doctrines, but rather because of allegations of moral breaches! Morris Cerullo, internationally renowned evangelist, in a 1991 teaching video program entitled **Manifested Sons of God**, made the following statements,

Jesus being the brightness of all that God has and is. He was the reflection, image, and manifestation visibly of all that God has and is. What is God's purpose and plan and objective? Sons and Daughters who will manifest all that God has and is. Can you imagine the power in your being when you face the devil? You represent all that God is and all that God has!

As if that didn't go far enough, Cerullo goes on in the video, to lead the congregation in the following blasphemous "confession,"

Everyone repeat after me...God is duplicating Himself in the earth...At last, the time has arrived, God is releasing His life through the Body [2 times]...Today, I am a Son of the all powerful Almighty God...The fullness of the Godhead dwells in me...God has planned for me to be Christ's image on earth.[12]

Few are as blatant as Morris Cerullo and Earl Paulk, but this is what the essence of Manifested Sons of God doctrine is, the deification of man.

Corporate Christ, Corporate Antichrist

To give you an idea of the extent of **this** kind of teaching, answer these questions. To whom does the scripture address, when God says, *Ask of me, and I will give you the heathen for thine inheritance?* Who is the one spoken of in Revelation 12 as "the manchild?" Whose responsibility is it to put the Enemies of God under Jesus' feet, subduing all things to Himself? The steady inroads the Manifested Sons of God teachers have made would lead many of us to answer the above doctrinal questions with "Why us, of course! The victorious church, the End Time Army." The correct answer of course is Jesus Christ! He alone is the one worthy, and in Him Psalm 2, Psalm 110, and Revelation 12 are fulfilled. He is the ultimate focus of all of the purposes of God!

The whole concept of Christ has been changed. The orthodox concept is that Jesus of Nazareth, one person, is Christ, the Lord's anointed. The revised gnostic concept is that because we are the Body of Christ, we are Christ! The corporate

Christ. Therefore, the things that scripture teach us Jesus Christ is going to accomplish, people are presumptuously taking upon themselves. Who is the church's one foundation? According to some Manifested Sons people, the answer is obvious, the apostles and prophets! Who's going to rule all the nations with a rod of iron? Who will execute judgement? Who is it that shall rule from the heavenlies administering protection, comfort and deliverance? The answer is obvious to anyone nourished on orthodox doctrine, but the Manifested Sons of God people have a different idea.

> The greatest decision that the church is going to have to make in these days ahead...is to face that there are apostles of God, that they must submit to that authority and to that office. They must submit to that foundation as though it was Jesus Christ, and whosoever will not submit to that authority shall be destroyed from among the people." (Royal Cronquist).[13]

> And this shaking is going to cast Satan and his principalities from their heavenly throne, while the Sons of God ascend into "the heavenlies," first of all in the Spirit—to take upon themselves the authority which belongeth to those who are overcomers. And entering this place of power and authority, the Sons of God shall be able to administer protection and comfort and help and deliverance to such as are in need.[14]

Can you see the subtle shift here? It is now **The Sons** of God who administer deliverance, throw Satan out of heaven, and enter a place of power and authority. Where is Jesus? I thought administering protection, deliverance, and help was His exclusive domain. Any authority we have, we didn't "take upon ourselves," it is delegated to us by He who alone is Sovereign!

If Christ is now corporate, so is Antichrist, in the new scheme of things. And where is Antichrist, or who is this spirit of Antichrist? Rick Joyner thinks it sits presently in the church! That is why he calls for a redefinition of Christianity!

> The change that is coming to the body of Christ is so profound that the world will have a new definition of Christianity...Those who submit to Him in truth...will be the most dangerous and powerful people on earth, and will be the greatest threat to the Antichrist spirit that now sits in the church as a substitute for Him. (Morningstar Journal, Vol 2, No. 1).

This may be why John Wimber thinks that Jesus is trying to get the church back (He lost it). According to the magazine, **Prophecy Today**:

> Vineyard Ministries International came to Britain. People were blessed, but the promised October revival did not take place...He (Wimber) testified to God having spoken to him concerning "the church." The word came, "tell them I have need of it." The issue, he said, is proprietorship or ownership. We don't own the church, Jesus does, and He wants it back. [When did He lose it?] As Jesus went into Jerusalem on the back of a donkey, so He will return on the back of a victorious church.[15]

Wimber echoes this allegorical "word" in a statement in "Zip to 3000 in 5 Years."

> The Lord spoke to me and said to me, "Just as I had need of the colt and the donkey for my entry into Jerusalem, I need my church back for my re-entry. Go to the church"...He gave me the impression that this was the message from now on. "The Lord hath need of it, the Lord wants His church back."[16]

Much of this error is brought in accompanied by a discontented, "not good enough yet" view of the church. We are told that the church has either a Jezebel spirit, or isn't united enough, and is whipped, defeated, waiting for the helicopter escape instead of getting down to the business of ruling and reigning (I can almost hear the Amens!). Marc DuPont, one of the leading "prophets" at Toronto Airport Vineyard, even went so far as to say, "God is bored with the church." Christians are being conditioned to hold to a very negative, critical, cynical view of the church, so they will be opened up to a radical redefinition of Christianity.

> ...The greatest test of the spirit of Antichrist is its attitude toward the church. The attitude isn't directed toward Jesus. Jesus is not personally a threat to any community unless there is a living thriving church functioning in that community. Therefore, the spirit of Antichrist refuses to recognize that God is here in the flesh.

Jewel Van der Merwe, in response says,

> Does that hit you? Now the true church is being called the spirit of Antichrist! The ones who do not have their eyes open now to see that the church is God here in the flesh now! Manifested Sons of God! Are you willing to accept that "we are to look for another?" Do you accept that the church now coming forth and being manifest is the coming of Christ we have been looking forward to since He ascended into heaven and Two men stood by them in white apparel; which also said Ye men of Galilee, why stand ye gazing up into heaven? This same Jesus which is taken up from you into heaven, shall so come in like manner as ye have seen Him go into heaven.[18]

Three Attributes of Manifested Sons of God

These three attributes seem to accompany this kind of teaching: (1) relentless attacks on the orthodox church; (2) a ridiculing of the Blessed Hope, the Rapture; (3) a reliance on allegory. There is an almost sarcastic presentation of the doctrinally orthodox church, as being "religious," dead, hypocritical, and escapist, this is reconditioning people to accept false doctrine.. Obviously, the church always stands in need of loving correction, however, to say that the spirit of Antichrist abides in her now, or that God is bored with her, goes way beyond reproof, into cynical attack.[19] We need to look at the church spiritually. Jesus loves the church, washes her constantly, and gives His life everyday for her. The true church doesn't need to manufacture unity, she has it. We are not defeated at all, we've overcome by the blood of the Lamb! Of course, looking at the institutional church would frustrate any sincere believer for remember, "Not all Israel is Israel." You can't even see the true church at all, unless God opens your eyes to her. Everywhere we travel we can find Christians. We have the blessed Koinonia of the Spirit already. While false teachers whine about the lack of unity, hoping to carnally manufacture it, we live in it.

I'm sure you can see by now the heavy reliance on allegorical preaching. Through allegory, you can make any point at all. That is not to say that we must never use allegory, but any doctrine whose only basis is allegory should be rejected. God speaks plainly and literally. The obvious meaning of a scripture is the one you should go by. The Bible wasn't written by mystics, nor is it for mystics. Only the childlike can receive His mysteries. Allegory has almost cast us into a mythological posture these days. We have people going to war against "Jezebel spirits" and "Ahab spirits." There are even people going forward to receive the "Jehu Anointing," and we are assured that Jezebel is still trying to kill the "prophets." What does this have to do with New Testament Christianity? At a time when we need more sobriety than ever, we are being misled into myths, legends, and vain imaginations! A major allegorization, that is commonly accepted is that all the feasts of Israel are "phases" that the church goes through, culminating in the Feast of Tabernacles, when God actually "comes to live among His people." Many believe that what is spontaneously happening the world over, is the Feast of Tabernacles.

Finally, Manifested Sons of God is relentless in its attacks on the eschatology which believes in "the rapture." It is ironic that the Manifested Sons of God, who believe that they can become immortal, and perfectly brought into the image of Christ, reject the action in which God actually does immortalize us. *We shall not all sleep but we shall all be changed, in a moment, in the twinkling of an eye...for this corruption must put on incorruption.* I guess they don't like the fact that God does it for us, not we ourselves through maturing, or gnosis (revelation). As Warnock says,

The church may proclaim an imminent rapture as much as they will and teach that any moment the saints will be snatched away from earth to escape the gathering clouds of the tribulation. But this is not the teaching of God's Word. True, we must be always waiting and watching for His appearing, but this is not the appearing of evangelical theology. This glorious appearing must first of all be manifest in the saints.[20]

There you have it, Jesus must come "within us," not necessarily for us, but a spiritualized "Second Coming." Rick Joyner goes even further when he says in his "The Harvest" prophecy:

The doctrine of the rapture was a great and effective ruse of the enemy to implant in the church a retreat mentality, but it will not succeed. Already this yoke has been cast off by the majority in the advancing church and it will soon be cast off by all...

What's the matter with the rapture? Nothing at all, when you have a heavenly agenda, a pilgrim mind set. But when you begin to say, *My Lord delays His coming* and develop an earthly agenda, (ruling, reigning, taking the world for Jesus, the government on the shoulders of super apostles), there remains nothing more than *eating and drinking with the drunken and beating the menservants and maidservants*. Because of this scripture, I look for the shepherding error to come back with a vengeance. Come quickly Lord Jesus.

In Conclusion

There is no "Manifested Sons of God" organization. What we are talking about is a philosophy, a redefined eschatology that centers around the church as being Christ in a corporate sense, and it is taking the prerogatives and responsibilities that are reserved for Jesus Christ, the person. Not everyone goes to the same extremes, as Earl Paulk, Royal Cronquist, or Morris Cerullo, but the presuppositions that led to those extremes are common. Those presuppositions; the corporate Christ concept, the ongoing incarnation, the rejection of God's rescue (the Rapture), the spiritualized "coming of Christ within," all of these and others are partly contributing to the atmosphere in which the Toronto Blessing can occur!

This is the context, coming from a foundation of Latter Rain, Manifested Sons of God, Charismatic excesses, "Word of Faith" teaching, Shepherding, Kingdom Now, and Dominion theology. Layer by layer the foundation has been laid, bringing us to the late 1980s and a church in the heartland of America, which put a spark to the general prophetic anticipation which had developed over the years by these influences.

End Notes

1. Richard Riss. "Latter Rain". Honeycomb Visual.

2. Franklin Hall. "Atomic Power With God Through Fasting and Prayer". Hall Deliverance Foundation. Among other things, Hall holds up as examples for Christians, American Indians praying to the Great Spirit, (they fast and it works!). He also advocates a Christian astrology, giving Christian interpretations of zodiacal signs and tells us that it was in "1848 AD, that the Aquarian Age was introduced to the world." He also taught that Jesus gave the secret teaching to some of the disciples, of being "gravity free!!" "Jesus taught a small, but precious group of His followers, those who were able to bear it, that gravity would be completely loosed from them, in the last days. When they learned how to train their appetites into a different channel. We must learn to labour for the meat that endures unto everlasting (immortal) life. The meat that draws us away from gravity holding things." Page 20. Hall also held an interesting view of Joel's army (Joel 2:3-11). From Page 55, "Gravity freed, great people will run up walls, not break rank, and if they fall on a sword, the immortality power from Jesus' body on them will protect them. It appears they also can walk or run upside down."

3. Al Dager. "Vengeance is Ours". Page 60.

4. Earl Paulk. Excerpt from "Joel's Army" by Jewel Van der Merwe.

5. Ibid. Bill Hamon. "The Eternal Church."

6. Bill Britton. "Jesus, the Pattern Son." Page 16.

7. Mike Bickle. Audio Tape. "Visions and Revelations."

8. John Wimber. Speaking, Docklands, England. October, 1990.

9. Bill Britton.

10. George Warnock. "Feast of Tabernacles." Page 46.

11. Ibid. Page 48.

12. Morris Cerullo Video. 1991. "Manifested Sons of God." I acknowledge Jewel's book "Joel's Army" for bringing this to my attention.

13. Royal Cronquist. Advertisement for speaking engagements.

14. Warnock. "Feast of Tabernacles." Page 35. According to Warnock, "The church is literally filled with carnal, earthly minded Christians who sit back in self complacency and await a rapture that will translate them out of earth's great tribulation at the beginning of the day of the Lord." Page 35.

15. Barry Killick. "Prophecy Today". Referring to October, 1990 meetings in England.

16. Wimber. "Zip to 3000 in 5 Years." Part I. Signs and Wonders Today. (Wheaton, IL, Christian Life Missions, 1983) Page 15.

17. Earl Paulk. "The Wounded Boy of Christ."

18. Jewel Van der Merwe. "Joel's Army." Page 23.

19. Warnock is particularly caustic at this point. "Feast of Tabernacles." Pages 36-37.

a. "As a whole, the church of Christ has suffered defeat from the powers of darkness for century upon century. Deceived on every hand, afflicted with all manner of sickness and disease, demon oppressed and demon possessed, filled with carnality, sin, bitterness, bewilderment, and sorrow, fear and torments. The surging masses of humanity, including many of the real saints of God, have been taken captive by the "god of this world," and instead of a glorious church, one needs only to visit a great healing meeting to behold a veritable museum of the devil, displaying his exhibits: children of God, twisted in the most gruesome forms, hobbling on crutches, dragging themselves, crawling on the ground, men with tortured minds, oppressed by demons and cast into Satan's mold of deception; fear, torment, filth...And yet, the saints really think they are telling the truth when they stand religiously on Sunday morning and sing to the charming peal of the organ. "Like a mighty army moves the church of God. Brothers we are treading where the saints have trod, One in hope and doctrine, one in charity, Onward Christian soldiers, Marching as to war...With the cross of

Jesus going to war." The exact opposite is just about the truth of the situation, a defeated band of slaves, divided into 1000 sects, all having different hopes and different doctrines and knowing nothing of charity."

b. What bitterness! But in a similar way, Manifested Sons of God teachers today continuously point to the discrepancies and short falls of the institutional church and say, "See. Look how divided we are…" Of course, I've been divided! But that's not even the point. All true Christians are united, by the Spirit! It takes the Spirit to see the bride of Christ, those who truly love Jesus and await His return. Do you think the apostles trashed the church the way these do? They offered much correction, but not in this disgusted spirit.

20. Warnock. "Feast of Tabernacles."

5
Anticipation for Revival

The "Blessed Hope" of the Church is He will indeed rescue us from the evils of this present age. This hope has been supplanted with a new "revelation." The new revelation is the perfecting of the church, the birthing of "manchild," and a worldwide revival, as the church comes into the fullness of Christ and exercises her dominion and authority. Christians have been conditioned to expect Christ to come "within" us, mystically, and to scoff at and reject the idea of Christ coming for us as being "the helicopter escape." Many Christians who have been influenced by dynamic and bold "prophets," have opted for a more optimistic scenario.

I too am optimistic, but for different reasons. Indeed, I look for the nations to stream to the mount of the Lord, and the glory of the Lord to cover the earth, as well as the healing of the nations. These things will be established by Jesus at His coming and not by a super-anointed church. I have to accept the Bible's teaching that in the end times, "All nations will hate you for my name's sake," even if it seems pessimistic. Nevertheless, Jesus will prevail, and in the process, we (the church) shall also. The basis for my belief is not mere optimism, it is rooted in an acceptance of scripture in its plain meaning.

Current Expectations

The following is an excerpt of a prophetic message which reflects the current optimism:

> Open your spiritual eyes even now and see that the Lord is forming His camp. And the camp of the Lord is very great. The voice of the Lord is uttered before His army and the army shall march! The army shall march! I tell you my people the army is going to march on the capitals of this nation. The army will gather around the capitals as a great band, and bind the powers of darkness and praise the name of the Lord and release the spirit of liberty upon this nation...And this nation is going to shake under the power of God. Take your eschatology and put it under your feet. Take my promises and let them be wings of victory. In your doctrine you have given yourselves little hope, but in my word I give you all hope. The best is in the future before you...say, "We shall overcome every wickedness of this nation."...You're going to see churches of 100s become churches of 1000s and churches of 1000s become churches of 10,000s. You are going to see whole cities where everybody comes together on Sunday morning—not just on Easter, but on a regular basis.[1]

Notice the Manifested Sons highlights, the "great" army on the march, binding the powers of darkness, and using their authority to "loose" the spirit of liberty on the nation. They love the idea of making the nation tremble! Make sure you throw out your eschatology, though, (especially the rapture) for the best is before us! Whole cities are going to come to God! Sounds a lot better than, "In the last day, many shall depart from the faith..." Which one is the most optimistic?

Ain't We Great?

In another more extensive (224 pages) prophecy, Rick Joyner can see the day coming when,

> The feet of the body of Christ will carry the credentials for all of those who have gone before them. They will be joined to each other like no other body of people have ever been joined, but they will be also joined to the true believers of all ages who lived and prophesied of this day. As Jesus promised, the things that He did and even greater things will be done in His name, because He went to the Father. His faithful will soon walk in unprecedented power and authority. In the near future, the church will not be looking back at the first century church with envy because of the great exploits of those days, but all will be saying that He certainly did save His best wine for last. The most glorious days in all of history have now come upon us. You who have dreamed of one day being able to talk to Peter, John and Paul are going to be surprised to find that they have been waiting to talk to you![2]

Do you notice the emphasis on greatness? But who, according to this scenario, is going to be great in those days? Not necessarily Jesus, nor even the first century church. The great ones are the last days, overcoming, manchild church! The early church can't wait to meet us! This nonsense is sheer Manifested Sons of God, church evolution theory.

Joyner goes on, though, to proclaim the day when,

> The magnitude of this harvest will ultimately astonish even the most optimistic believers. Congregations of less than a hundred will be adding a thousand believers a week for periods of time. Meetings which begin spontaneously will stir entire cities, continuing until they fill the largest stadiums night after night. Previously popular sporting events will be abandoned in many regions for lack of interest. Whole towns with populations of thousands will swarm on neighbouring towns to evangelize them...News teams will follow apostles like national figures...large cities will experience periods of zero crime...pornography, prostitution, illegal drugs, abortion, and drunkenness will cease to exist in many areas without passage of a single law...Whole nations will give themselves to periods of fasting and prayer.[3]

When? Before or after Jesus returns?

I realize, at this point, that I risk being perceived as a negative, maybe even cynical person. The reality is that there isn't a Christian alive who wouldn't long for these things to happen, but on what terms? Are we to imagine that the church will affect these things in the period of time before the return of Jesus? The new "prophets" seem to imply that it is **We** who will do all this (of course, in the power of God). But what does the Bible teach? Even though they seem pessimistic, don't the prophecies of the New Testament count for anything? False prophets have finally gotten us to the point of saying, *My Lord delayeth in coming.*

Luke 12:40 Be ye therefore ready also: for the Son of man cometh at an hour when ye think not.

I Tim 4:1-2 Now the Spirit speaketh expressly, that in the latter times some shall depart from the faith, giving heed to seducing spirits, and doctrines of devils; Speaking lies in hypocrisy; having their conscience seared with a hot iron.

II Tim 3:1-5 This know also, that in the last days perilous times shall come. For men shall be lovers of their own selves, covetous, boasters, proud, blasphemers, disobedient to parents, unthankful, unholy, without natural affection, trucebreakers, false accusers, incontinent, fierce, despisers of those that are good, traitors, heady, highminded, lovers of pleasures more than lovers of God; Having a form of godliness, but denying the power thereof: from such turn away.

It's becoming obvious, the extent of the conditioning that we have undergone, when you think about the ridiculous "prophecy" uttered on **Trinity Broadcasting Network,** to the effect that on Thursday, June 9th, 1994, "all evil would be ripped off the face of the earth." This prophecy actually created quite an excitement, being endorsed by Paul Crouch and confirmed by other prophetic voices. As you know, nothing anywhere near that happened on June 9th. The only explanation, of course, was a spiritualization (something about a spiritual veil being removed) – obviously a false prophet (Deut 13 and 18). But why would we even have to wait till June to judge it? Such an obviously unscriptural notion (that evil will be suddenly ripped off the face of the earth, but not by the Second Coming) should have been dismissed as nonsense, as soon as it was uttered! This shows us the tremendous extent of Manifest Sons theology. To them, it is the wicked, not the righteous, who would be removed!

This is a very disturbing development. When the rapture happens, the devil will offer a plausible excuse, one way or the other. He will have to either say that people at random disappeared, or it was the wicked who were taken. Already within the New Age Movement, there is an idea that when the world makes its "quantum leap" into an evolved consciousness, those so narrow minded as to believe that there is only one way of salvation, will have to be removed. Only after that can the new day of enlightenment and tolerance dawn.

I Thess 4:16-18 For the Lord himself shall descend from heaven with a shout, with the voice of the archangel, and with the trump of God: and the dead in Christ shall rise first: Then we which are alive and remain shall be caught up together with them in the clouds, to meet the Lord in the air: and so shall we ever be with the Lord. Wherefore comfort one another with these words.

Luke 21:34-36 And take heed to yourselves, lest at any time your hearts be overcharged with surfeiting, and drunkenness, and cares of this life, and so that day come upon you unawares. For as a snare shall it come on all them that dwell on the face of the whole earth. Watch ye therefore, and pray always, that ye may be accounted worthy to escape all these things that shall come to pass, and to stand before the Son of man.

Obviously, the scriptures teach that the true believer will be removed and the wicked will be left.

What About the Wheat and the Tares?

Good question. The parable in Matt 13 has been interpreted to teach that at the end of time, it will be the tares (wicked) removed and then the righteous will shine forth. On this basis many are rejecting their traditional hope, the gathering together (rapture). Just remember that in that parable we are not told that the tares are removed and burned first, we are told that they are **bound together** first, for the purpose of burning, and then the wheat is gathered. This binding of the tares is actually happening right now in the current ecumenism. See endnote seven for expanded treatment of Matthew 13.

In one way, the false prophet who predicted something for June 9th, may well be on to something. It does seem that from that time on there has been an increase in these mystical outbreaks spawned by Toronto and Rodney Howard Browne! Suddenly, they exploded worldwide! Perhaps the June prophecies were to be a signal of increased delusion and false experience, for those under judgement.

There have been others who claim to be "prophets" of God who pointed to June, 1994. One example is Kim Clement, who was a guest of the Trinity Broadcasting Network in April, 1994. In an interview with both Paul Crouch and his son Matthew, Kim gave a "word" which according to Paul Crouch, nearly "lifted them out of their chairs." Here is an excerpt,

The Spirit of the Lord says, I will raise up a brand new and a fresh and powerful anointing that is going to destroy and expose hidden works of darkness...Thus says the Lord, get ready, for even as the enemy tries to destroy and bring addictions and witchcraft upon the nation, so liberty and revival is about to take place as you have never seen. For this is the final move of my spirit. This is the final thing that I am preparing for your hearts to do. Therefore, get ready, says the Lord, I am about to change you with my power and anointing...Surely I am about to judge from the very top, says the Lord, and this judgement has already begun and will not go by June before it is absolutely done, says the Lord...Therefore, take it now, take my word and rejoice for I will bring about the greatest move of the Spirit that this nation has ever seen...[4]

Notice, Clement prophesied powerful things! There's going to be an anointing, so fresh and powerful, exposing darkness, and revival is coming like never before, but then, amazingly a specific word! God would begin to judge, starting at the top and by the end of June His judgement would be absolutely done! (I assume he's talking about a judgement of God's people). Are you kidding? God has judged His people and it's over? Has anyone at all called Clement or Crouch on this false prophecy?

Strong Delusion

It's time to take seriously the warning of II Thess 2:1-11, that God would send a strong delusion upon those who receive not the love of the truth. Does the Bible teach what the Manifest Sons are prophesying? There will always be sporadic revivals. There are revivals happening all over the world. However, are we to expect a great, earth shattering, end-time revival, where the nations fall at our feet? Or is that wishful thinking (and prophesying)? There will be a revival indeed, and one with signs and wonders, on a worldwide scale, but it will be a mystical, sensuous, lying revival, in the "deceivableness of unrighteousness after the working of Satan."

Not According to Ken Copeland

But Ken Copeland, in the June, 1994, **Believers Voice of Victory** assures us,

Can you imagine somebody walking around with the power that Elisha and Elijah had and the power that Peter and Paul had—all at the same time? It's about to happen! If you'll get your act straightened up and get yourselves moving in the Spirit of God, it will happen to you!...I asked the Lord one time, "Lord how will you do that? How can you make the sun not shine?" He told me He will block out its light with the cloud of His glory...God said to me, "I'll make that cloud get so thick on whole cities, that people can't see the sunshine." Then, He added, "That's the reason you need to get ready"...Learn [how to win souls] because when God's power falls and His glory cloud hits a whole city at one time, men and women will fall under the power of it, crying out to God.[5]

Copeland then promises us that "thousands of people will come running to those churches. God will give us whole cities at once. Not only that, this move of the Spirit will grow until we get whole nations flowing into the mountain of God." Copeland closes his "prophetic" article with this "word" from God.

The Lord said to me, I've been manifest as the rain, I've been manifest as the fire, or lightning. I've been manifest as the wind, but I've never been manifest as all four at the same time. Now, in the time of the former and latter rain, you're going to see all of me for the first time ever.[6]

Do you really think that God said that to Ken Copeland? We are finally going to see "all of" Him now, for the first time ever? Remember, we aren't talking about the beatific vision of I John 3:1-3 here.

I John 3:1-3 Behold, what manner of love the Father hath bestowed upon us, that we should be called the sons of God: therefore the world knoweth us not, because it knew him not. Beloved, now are we the sons of God, and it doth not yet appear what we shall be: but we know that, when he shall appear, we shall be like him; for we shall see him as he is. And every man that hath this hope in him purifieth himself, even as he is pure.

These men are teaching and prophesying to us that this will come to pass in these days, before the coming of the Lord, in the great end-time revival! Sounds good, but did the apostles believe that way?

Revival as a Sovereign Act of God

I was "raised" to have this expectation, through my Christian life. Being saved in an Assembly of God church, I was taught to expect the imminent return of Jesus Christ. Having that hope was a purifying effect on my life. But shortly after my salvation, I was given a twelve tape album, "Spirit, Soul and Body," by Kenneth Copeland. I devoured them, and became immersed in "The Faith Message." I don't believe that Faith teachers deny the rapture, as a rule. But they do stress that "victory is up to us" and "you can have what you say." It's easy to conclude, "Why should we go out of this earth as a whipped, sick and defeated church? We can go out in victory!" Well, I do agree that we don't have to be whipped, sick or defeated. But what is victory? When Noah went on the ark with only his family, was he defeated? He preached for 120 years without converts, was he whipped? Why didn't he just have a great pre-flood revival? Revival belongs to God. One time I was singing, "There's going to be a revival in the land, in the land, there's going to be a revival in the land, from the north, to the south, to the east, and the west, there's going to be a revival, there's going to be a revival, there's going to be a revival in the land!" in church one day, and I heard this word, "presumptuous!" We presume that there is, but on what basis? Where in the Bible are we led to expect an earth shattering, hospital emptying, nation converting, universal revival? When the apostles told us about the last days, is that the picture they painted? Or, are you going more by William Branham, Ken Copeland, and Paul Cain? I can hope and pray for revival, I believe there will always be sporadic, local revivals, but the truth is, there may never be another revival in America. Does that make God unjust? Has He not given us revival? Do we have any excuse? Don't get me wrong, hope and pray for revival, but don't presumptuously assume, "There's going to be a revival in the land," as if God's Word guarantees it. *The wind bloweth where it listeth.* God can do whatever He pleases, He is not beholden to us.

Through the 1980s and into the 1990s, I have seen the expectation build, "God is going to do something dramatic, there is going to be an explosion of miracles! Christians are going to run everything. Hospitals are going to be emptied, whole nations will turn to the church, prophets are going to advise presidents, etc. etc." We've heard the messages and prophecies.

Only by acknowledging and understanding this expectation, can we begin to understand Toronto and put it in context. There has been a conditioning, a change in view of the last days, a heavenly expectation has been usurped by a worldly, earthly, even sensuous/religious expectation. And it looks like that expectation is finally beginning to be fulfilled, thanks to two major ministries. The **thrust** into the "Mystical Revival" is directly related to the Kansas City Prophets, also the ministry of John Wimber and the Vineyard Movement. The **catalyst** can be attributed to Rodney Howard Browne. All of these and their contribution to Toronto and the world is what we will look at next.

End Notes

1. Glenn Foster. Excerpt of prophecy given July 11, 1994. "Fields of Honey." Sweetwater Church of the Valley. Box 5640, 1420 43rd Avenue, Glendale, AZ 85312.
2. Rick Joyner. "The Harvest." Page 26.
3. Ibid. Page 32-33.
4. Trinity Broadcasting Network. April, 1994.
5. Kenneth Copeland. "A Storm of Glory." Believers Voice of Victory. June, 1994.
6. Ibid.
7. Matthew 13, or the parables of the kingdom of God, is a collection of parables about the progress of the kingdom of God on the earth. All these parables belong together, examining the subject from different angles. The essence of the Matthew 13 parables is this, that of all of the multitudes in the sphere of the kingdom of God, there is actually only a remnant of genuine believers and there is coming a separation.

•   In the parable of the sower, of the four different soils (hearts) that the seed (the Word) was planted in, only one bore fruit.

•   In the wheat and the tares, of all the plants in the vast field, a good number were tares and not wheat. They would have to be separated. Both were to grow together till the time of the harvest (end of the age). The instruction was "gather together first the tares, bind them in bundles, to burn them," then harvest the wheat. What stage are we in now? The stage of gathering together the tares (ecumenism) for the purpose of burning.

•   The mustard plant—was fine as an herb, growing at the rate that it was to grow. But when there came a rapid unnatural acceleration, two things happened. The fowls of the air came (demons Matt 13:4) to lodge in its branches (division, denominations). How much of the tree is actual? What is in that tree that doesn't belong there? What part of the growth was real, and what wasn't?

•   In the parable of the leaven, the woman hides the leaven in the lump. (There are certain men crept in unawares). Leaven is corruption and false teaching. The result? A flat cake becomes a huge loaf! But how much of that puffed up loaf is actually bread and how much is air? The loaf looks huge, but is actually light!

•   The treasure in the field—The man (Jesus Christ) sells everything he has, to obtain the field. Why does he want the field? He doesn't. He wants the treasure in the field, but he has to buy it all, the whole package. Even so did our Lord die for all men, believer and unbeliever alike, but his real desire is for the treasure to come out of the field. Even so, a separation is coming, the treasure that he sold out to obtain, is going to be taken out of the field.

•   In another parable about pearls, of all the pearls and jewels the merchant had, they were not like the one great pearl. There had to be a separation, he had to sell all of the rest of them to obtain the pearl of great price.

•   In the parable of the dragnet—a huge harvest of fish is brought to the shore, to be separated. Of all the "converts" brought in, how many are real? How many will be rejected? An ultimate judgement is ahead.

    In each case, it is the good, the valuable and worthwhile which is taken out, from among the false and worthless.

6
The Kansas City Prophets

Inside a Prophetic Service

The "prophet" had the crowd following every word he said, even almost every movement he made, in fact, every sensation he felt in his body!

[Bob Jones] Hmmmm, witchcraft coming again...check that in Jesus' name. I feel pin pricks on me. There's witchcraft comin'...

Then the pastor, Mike Bickle explains to the crowd,

When Bob feels pin pricks in his hand, that just show up, that means witchcraft is in this [place]...The phrase that Bob uses is his senses turn golden...His five senses are literally inspired by the Holy Spirit ...He could tell what was happening in the spirit realm from the five senses...[1] (See *Jude 19*)

What's going on here? No, it's not a psychic, it's a full gospel church service, featuring Mike Bickle and "seer" Bob Jones! Bob Jones is "picking up" witchcraft by the pin prickly feeling in his hand and Mike Bickle is asking him to elaborate on the whole concept of "golden senses," in which 20-30 different signs show up in his physical body to help him divine the spiritual realm. For example, his hands turn different colours to indicate things, (purple-royalty, red-intercession, etc). Did the apostles ever model anything even remotely like this? Never mind, these men are part of the new breed, they are so anointed that the apostles can't wait to meet them! As Mike Bickle says,

The saints in the New Testament would wait in line to greet the apostles coming from this generation![2]

Who Are the Kansas City Prophets?

In following the trail of error that has led to this current mystic revival, we need to fully explore the role of the company of men known as the Kansas City Prophets. The controversy that surrounded them in the late 1980s and very early 1990s seems to have died down since John Wimber came forward to offer them a "covering" through affiliation with the Vineyard Movement. It is my contention that instead of truly resolving the problems that were raised by these false prophets, a band-aid was put over the whole affair. The erroneous teaching and ministry of Paul Cain, Bob Jones, John Paul Jackson, and others has been promoted and circulated through the Body of Christ in the years since Vineyard has been their covering. Bob Jones, (one of the more obviously false prophets) finally was exposed, but not as a false prophet, but for an ethical/moral failure. His prophecies have been cited several times as valid at Toronto Airport Vineyard. The same people who heralded these men as prophets are now heralding this spiritual drunkenness as a great "end times" revival. Perhaps behind the scenes of this "latest move of the Spirit" there just might be some of the same people offering their "prophetic ministry." We are not talking about personality differences or about doctrinal hairsplitting. The men I'll be discussing in this chapter have presumed to speak prophetically, in the name of the Lord, (as though God were talking) to the whole, universal church! They have made great claims, like "The Lord spoke to me clearly..." or "I stood face to face before the Lord." And what is in the message? Sheer Manifested Sons, Latter Rain, last days Super Church, church as the "manchild" stuff, reheated, repackaged and rehashed!

In describing the Kansas City Prophets, there are three men, Mike Bickle, Bob Jones, and Paul Cain who held the most prominence. It's also important, however, to take a fresh look at how the church handled (or failed to handle with responsibility) the exposure of false prophecy, for this has set the course which we are currently on, and the same people who wouldn't discern at that time, even more so now, refuse to think critically.

Mike Bickle

Mike Bickle is the pastor of a church in Kansas City, Missouri, "the heartland of America." The church is now known as the Metro Vineyard of Kansas City. In the early 1980s it was called KCF for Kansas City Fellowship. Bickle originally had pastored in St. Louis. In June of 1982, a man named Augustine approached Bickle and told him that he had heard an audible voice telling him to prophesy by the "spirit of truth" to Bickle's congregation. Bickle allowed him to do this and was impressed by the seeming accuracy with which he described the condition of his church. In September, the same year, Mike Bickle himself heard an audible voice speak to him, while on a trip in Cairo, Egypt. The voice told him,

I am inviting you to raise up a work that will touch the ends of the earth. I have invited many people to do this thing and many people have said yes, but very few have done my will.[3]

Shortly after this, on a "word from the Lord," Bickle went to pastor a small group in Kansas City, Missouri. The church grew rapidly in a very short time. In 1986, Bickle and his elders formed an organization called Grace Ministries, which they described as, "A ministry team of men committed to seeing the church fully restored to the glory described in God's Word."[4] Now, Grace Ministries and KCF are two distinct organizations. Al Dager gives a good description of the function of Grace Ministries,

Grace Ministries is a parachurch organization that represents several men who engage in itinerant, allegedly prophetic, ministries...There are seven major facets to Grace Ministries: 1. Apostolic teams; 2. City churches; 3. The House of Prayer; 4. The Joseph Company; 5. The Israel Mandate; 6. A Ministry training center; 7. Shiloh Ministries.[5]

I won't try to describe in detail each facet, as Al Dager did in his helpful **Media Spotlight Report**, but I will highlight a few aspects of two of the facets.

• **City churches,** Bickle believes that every city really only has one church, which may consist of several congregations, but must come under one, citywide, eldership. As **Ministries Today** reported,

Bickle and his leadership team have promoted a concept advocating unity among all pastors in a geographic area. Bickle now says that the idea should have emphasized "unity through friendship" rather than "unity through a church government structure." Many pastors in Kansas City felt threatened by what they perceived to be an attempt to "swallow" other churches under KCF's banner. "The way we used terminology created fear, division, and suspicion," Bickle admits.[6]

• **Shiloh Ministries** was or is, the development of a prophetic community. A piece of land was designated and developed, where prophets could live together, convene prophetic conferences, share their insights, and train up other prophets. The senior prophetic authority recognized over Shiloh, was to be Paul Cain, a former associate of William Branham. Cain once called Branham, "The greatest prophet who ever lived." [It is interesting to note that there was, in Iowa, (might still be) a "prophetic" retreat and community called Shiloh. It was noted for its Manifested Sons of God teaching. This was founded by John Robert Stevens, of "The Walk."]

Though Bickle is the pastor of KCF and founder of Grace Ministries, he at one point, seemed to back down from calling anybody a prophet. Here is an excerpt from an interview he had with Al Dager.

There's no one in our midst that we give the title "prophet." The only one I would feel comfortable of giving that office would be Paul Cain, but he refuses to accept it. So, I'd say both of them, apostle and prophet—I believe that in God's purpose they exist, but we're very hesitant to designate somebody as being one at this point and time.[7]

But on the other hand, in his lengthy interview with Bob Jones on the tape, "Visions and Revelations," Jones describes numerous face to face encounters with the Lord. Upon Bickle's encouragement, Jones tells the crowd what God supposedly said, what he saw in the throne room, what he clearly "heard." If that is not playing the role of the prophet, what is? Semantically avoiding the actual title "prophet," but then delivering messages to the church in the name of the Lord, seems hypocritical to me. To avoid the scrutiny of Deut 13 and Deut 18, they call themselves "prophetic ministries" instead of "prophets." But even the ones who follow them know better, calling them "The Prophets."

I believe that Mike Bickle has been zealous, and well intentioned. I have read a book of his, **Passion for Jesus**, which makes clear some beautiful teachings about the attributes of God, the fear of the Lord, and knowing God. But I also believe that through an unfortunate lack of discernment, he has promoted false prophets, as well as the doctrines of Manifested Sons of God, on an international scale. This has helped pave the way for the current mysticism. The next person we will discuss is an excellent example of this.

Bob Jones

Bob Jones has been described publicly at KCF as a "resident seer." This is unfortunate because he turned out to be one of the most blatant examples of a false prophet. How anyone can listen to him for even 10 minutes and not completely reject him as a prophet, is amazing! Yet, Mike Bickle and KCF thought enough of him to tape a lengthy interview with him called, "Visions and Revelations." The blatantly false doctrine, and occultic dreams and "revelations" found on this tape were enabled to make their way all over the world in a relatively short time. On the tape, Jones describes how he went from being a drunkard, fornicator, and bar room brawler, to eventually land in a mental institution, where he was regularly visited by demons who would hold conversations with him. Finally, Jesus Himself told Bob in order to get his mind back, to either kill or forgive twelve people he hated! Jones goes on to describe his Christian life and supernatural ministry.

One unforgettable episode that Jones recounts is how he received a visit from an angelic guide name "Dominus." "Dominus" eventually turned out to be the Lord Jesus Christ Himself, according to Jones. Jones tells how, in an out of body experience, he and Dominus sat above the KCF "in the Spirit," on rocking chairs, holding hands. To confirm Jones' "ministry" to Mike Bickle and his brother in law and associate pastor Bob Scott, Dominus revealed to Jones that he would visit the two men in their dreams. Each man subsequently had a dream in which a friend they knew named "Don" appeared (two separate Don's). When they asked Jones why Don appeared and not Jesus, Jones impatiently replied,

You guys are never going to learn the language of the Spirit, are you?...Jesus appears in thousands of different faces to portray something. He was trying to say, "I'm your friend, I am your familiar friend and I'm going to show you all things so you can move in the power of the Spirit."[8]

To be honest with you, I think this was a combination of the working of a powerful familiar spirit and incredible naivety. Bickle would later say of Jones, "He should have had a backstage ministry."[9]

The Shepherd's Rod

Bob Jones also contributed the Shepherd's Rod Revelation to the Body. According to him, "Everyone must pass under the shepherd's rod once a year." It all started when, according to Mike Bickle,

> Ten years ago, the Lord began to visit Bob and tell him that he would visit him on the day of atonement each year...The Lord literally stands before Bob and speaks to him...it's a real holy thing before the Lord...[10]

"The Lord" showed Bob Jones that on the day of atonement the shepherd of the congregation must hold out his staff and all must pass under it for a time of prophetic inspection. If they are in sin, it will be revealed prophetically to the leader. Bob Jones says this is a time where the Lord turns you upside down and looks you over for blemishes. Thus, through this blatant denial of the cross, you have God's people observing a distorted day of atonement.

It would take an entire book to catalogue the heresy of this one man, and that is not my purpose. My burden in this chapter is to remind us, where was the discernment? We were so spiritual, so full of "mystical" revelation and "cutting edge truth," but look at what we overlooked! The emperor obviously has no clothes! And when it began to be exposed by Ernie Gruen, it was almost dealt with as a matter of personal animosity and covered over. These men didn't leave ministry, their tapes weren't pulled. They haven't missed a beat! This is why we are so blind and intoxicated right now. Before there was a scandal, Mike Bickle said of Bob Jones, "There is nobody in the natural that had a more integral role in establishing our foundations in that kind of prophetic way, than Bob [Jones]"[11] After part of the controversy, Mike Bickle expresses regrets, "I made the mistake of allowing Bob Jones to step out from backstage into prominent, public ministry," and "I believe the Lord gave Bob Jones a backstage ministry, but I promoted him on the front stage."[12] Backstage ministry? I hope not. I'd rather have people like him out in the open than influencing movements backstage. Here are just a few of the blatant errors promoted by the "backstage ministry."

• When Bob Scott, associate pastor at KCF questioned Bob Jones about being in a recent dream, Jones replied, "It was not a dream, it was something other than a dream." He questioned Jones again, "Was that a dream or a trance or a vision?" Bob says, "Well, it was neither, I was there...on occasions, I'm there, it's not a vision, it's not a trance, I'm there."[13]

• Bob Jones' White Talking Horse—(Bob Jones) "The first time I ever seen the white horse was when an angel called Gabriel was riding. I saw him a couple of times in the '70s, I didn't understand what it meant, I would just see the white horse...(Mike Bickle interjects) (Mike Bickle) "The white horse always speaks in Bob's visions...In his vision it speaks of the corporate purpose that God is bringing to pass..."[14]

•   35 Super Apostles like unto Paul—Bob Jones saw and described a vision in which, "The Holy Spirit took me to a place—this time it wasn't the Lord took me, it was the Holy Spirit. He took me to a place and I saw the Lord, high and lifted up, by some young men and he set upon the golden ark...and I looked and there were men that had hold of the ark and they had the ark upon their shoulders. And the government will be upon their single shoulders." Jones goes on to explain how, by way of allegory, the Lord showed him he would raise up 35 men, to be champions for Christ in the last days. "...They will reign and reveal to the world that they truly are the faithful and true leaders and the government that will be upon his single shoulder." Mike Bickle comments, "I think there'll be 35 like unto Paul...There would be 35 whom the Lord would separate in the highest way. The government rests on apostles and prophets."[15]

What a perversion of Isaiah 9, in which Jesus is described as *Wonderful, Counsellor, the mighty God, the everlasting Father* and *the one on whose shoulder shall rest the government of the whole earth*!! Yet how typical of Manifested Sons heresy, to replace the person of the Lord Jesus Christ, with the "corporate Christ" concept.

•   Bob's revelation concerning prophetic accuracy. Bob Jones, in the tape "Shepherd's Rod" told us that God had revealed to him that the Rhema (spoken word) would be two-thirds accurate in the days to come. In other words, up to two-thirds of the time these prophets would be "right on." Why not 100% of the time? If you listen to Bob Jones, you would be glad for inaccurate prophets! Why? God showed Bob, supposedly, that if enough power was released to give us 100% accuracy, we would have dead Ananias' and Sapphira's all over the place! (How's that for making people actually thankful for inaccurate prophets?) Jones says we shouldn't worry about inaccurate prophesies, for God told him that prophets are like guns and prophecies are like bullets and inaccurate prophecies are like blanks. And he also says that God told him, "I'm loading the guns, I'm putting the blanks in!" Incredible! Jones would have us believe that God is responsible for inaccurate prophecies! Supposedly, even when we shoot blanks, it scares the enemy! Bob Jones complains about people who "try to make us Old Testament prophets" meaning to hold them to the standard of Deut 18. He then quotes I Cor 14, about giving prophecy in church and judging to see if they are all right.

There is a huge difference in giving a prophecy, "To edify, exhort, and comfort" the church, and in being a prophet, who presumes to speak in the name of the Lord. But we aren't trying to make these modern "prophets" into Old Testament prophets, they are. They are the ones who emphatically say, "The Lord said this," or "I saw the Lord face to face, and He said thus and so..." that's a far cry from supernatural utterance to edify, exhort, and comfort. Standing up and making bold pronouncements to the church universal in the name of God is a serious matter, New or Old Testament. Leading the church into error as a teacher is bad enough, but to claim direct revelation while doing it is even worse. Bob Jones is a man who claims to have five to six visions and revelations per day. We are talking about a man who thought he was a backslider when two days went by without a visitation from Jesus. He actually stands before the Lord on the day of atonement, remember? And Mike Bickle enthusiastically promoted it!

• The New Breed To Come, The Elected Seed—Bob Jones has much to say about the actual bloodline of the great last days overcomers. Bob reports that the Lord told him, "From out of the sands of time I have called the best of every bloodline in the earth, unto this generation...Even the bloodline of Paul...of David...of Peter, James and John, the best of their seed is unto this generation. They will even be superior to them in heart, stature and love for me..." What does bloodline matter to God, *who of one blood, made us all?* Sounds more like some kind of Eugenics cult than the gospel of Jesus Christ. Jones goes on to promise prophetically, the old Manifested Sons of God hopes that, "They will move into things of the supernatural that no one has ever moved in before. Every miracle, sign and wonder that has ever been in the Bible, they'll move in it consistently. They'll move in the power that Christ did...They themselves will be that generation that's raised up to put death itself underneath their feet and to glorify Christ in every way...So that glorious church might be revealed in the last days because the Lord Jesus is worthy to be lifted up by a church that has reached the full maturity of the God man!"[16]

This is typical of the sheer Manifested Sons heresy promoted by KCF and Grace Ministries. Has anyone renounced this? No, they renounce the fact that they put Bob Jones out in "front stage" and not "backstage," but the heresy isn't rejected. Jones' real problem was that he openly promoted things that others realize the church isn't "quite ready for."

Several times while I have been in Toronto at the Airport Vineyard, the prophecies of Bob Jones were discussed in a non-critical matter, as having been fulfilled in part by this revival. In a transcript of a meeting at Airport Vineyard, Friday, October 14, 1994, Wes Campbell discusses Bob Jones' revelation of an upcoming "civil war" in the church. In this war, the blue represents "revelation knowledge" people, fighting for freedom in the Spirit. "The grey" as in grey matter, those bound to their minds, you know, critical thinking (of course they are the ones keeping the church in slavery). This "revelation" was discussed as being credible and soon coming.[17]

This failure to resolve to correct the obvious lack of discernment, has cost us our spiritual eyesight, and led us deeper into error. Bob Jones can be an object lesson to us. After all, how could all of the "great prophetic company" fail to "pick up on him?" Truly, the emperor has no clothes.

Rev 3:17-18 Because thou sayest, I am rich and increased with goods, and have need of nothing; and knowest not that thou are wretched, and miserable, and poor, and blind, and naked: I counsel thee to buy of me gold tried in the fire, that thou mayest be rich; and white raiment, that thou mayest be clothed, and that the shame of thy nakedness do not appear; and anoint thine eyes with eyesalve, that thou mayest see.

Paul Cain

One of the most prominent and well received ministries associated with KCF is the ministry of Paul Cain. The people of KCF and Grace Ministries have held Cain in the highest regard.

> We [KCF] have recognized a mandate from the Lord to make a special commitment to follow the leadership of John Wimber and Paul Cain. Grace Ministries believes that these two men are chosen vessels among others in the nation.[18]

In the tape, "Visions and Revelations" in which Bickle interviews Bob Jones, Cain is described by Jones as "the most anointed prophet that's in the world today." He is said to have the "fear mantle on him," and we are assured that "the enemy would love to take him out before he [Cain] anoints this next generation, before he writes upon your mind...before he imparts his anointing into thousands of you."[19]

Paul Cain has an interesting background. In his testimony, it is reported that immediately before his birth, his mother was nearly dead from four major conditions. Breast cancer, tuberculosis, heart disease, and three other malignant tumours, all of which were afflicting her at the time she was to give birth. But an angel of the Lord came to her and told her not to fear, she would not die, but give birth to a male child. The angel even told her to name him Paul for he would preach the gospel as Paul did. As you can see, there are many similarities to the testimony of William Branham—with whom Cain was to one day be an associate. Paul Cain says that the angel of the Lord spoke to him at the age of eight in an audible voice. "I heard an audible voice and of course, often the angel of the Lord—it might have been the Lord Jesus Christ—but anyway, when He speaks it's rather awesome."[20]

Joel's Army

Paul Cain testifies of another unusual visitation which occurred at the age of 19, which gave him a message that he still promotes. An angel appeared to him in glory and magnificence, holding out a sword, pointing to a billboard. The billboard said, "Joel's army now in training." When he asked the Lord what it meant, the Lord took him through the book of Joel. Joel's army is described in Joel 2:1-11. To Cain and others, Joel's army is that great last days church, that "New Breed" of believers in whom the whole plan of God is climaxed in. These are the ones who take the world for Christ, are in perfect unity, invincible, and even divine in a sense! The idea of a Joel's army of invincible saints, executing judgement, is an outstanding example of the Latter Rain/Manifested Sons of God teachers.

In 1947, Paul Cain began a public healing ministry, he was 18 years old. His contemporaries were William Branham, Oral Roberts, A. A. Allen, Jack Coe, T. L. Osborne, etc. As the healing revival exploded and prosperity and popularity increased Cain saw greed, pride, and self service begin to characterize himself and others he knew. He entered into a season of repentance of which he would say after that God stripped everything away. It was during that season of repentance that he had another life changing visitation from the Lord,

> God had told him that if he kept himself from corruption and remained content with living a humble life, marked by scripture study and prayer, one day he would be allowed to stand before a *new breed* of men and women leaders. These would be marked by simplicity, purity, and remarkable manifestations of power.[21]

Thus began 25 years of extremely low profile for this "prophet" of the Lord, whom the Lord had also called to be celibate. It wasn't until April of 1987 that "the Lord ordained a divine appointment for Paul with Mike Bickle and others from KCF"[22] "The KCF eldership instantly felt the Lord prompting them to make a deep and permanent commitment to serve Paul Cain in anyway possible for the rest of his days as the Lord permitted."[23] Bob Jones, the "resident seer" at KCF went so far as to say of Cain, "The Lord named Paul Cain's ministry, 'The Terror of the Lord' or 'The Jealousy of God.'"[24]

Terror of the Lord? What is it about Paul Cain that causes people to regard him so reverently? Paul Cain has exhibited the ability to tell people the details of their lives, hidden sins and even things they have said in confidence to others. There have been reports of earthquakes and other natural disasters predicted by him.

> In January of 1989, Paul Cain told Jack Deere, a Vineyard pastor, that an earthquake would occur on the day Paul arrived for the first time to meet John Wimber at the church in Anaheim, California. Another would occur elsewhere in the world the day after he left Anaheim. Cain said that the earthquake would be a confirmation that the Lord had a strategic purpose for the Vineyard Movement. The first earthquake took place in Pasadena on the day Cain arrived. He left Anaheim on December 7. The Soviet-Armenian earthquake occurred on December 8.[25]

Another reason that Paul Cain is highly regarded as a "Terror of the Lord" could be the reported power surges of electricity that occur at places where he ministers. On one occasion in a church a tremendous surge of electrical power blew out circuits and set off fire alarms. The fire department responded, only to find that there was no fire, just a "prophetic meeting!" In Anaheim, California, even a battery operated video camera was short circuited, and the telephone systems were "blown out!" People have attributed this to the "heavy prophetic anointing" on Paul Cain, but does this sound like the Holy Spirit moving to you?

Not every manifestation is heavy or frightening as Clifford Hill points out in his review of **Some Said It Thundered**, a book defending the Kansas City Prophets.

The main body of this book is an account of story after story of what I believe are best described as "paranormal experiences," such as the following telephone conversation between Paul Cain...and Mike Bickle. After the opening greetings Paul Cain said, "Why Mike, you've got a bit of a sniffle and you are all wet. Your hair is standing up on the left side of your head." Bickle called his wife, Diana, to look at him. "Sweetheart, Paul says I have a sniffle, I am all wet, and my hair is standing up on one side. Am I all wet?" "Yes," she said, "You've just come out of the shower." "And is my hair standing up on one side?" "Yes," she replied, "on the left side!" Paul Cain calls these strange experiences little tokens that the line is still open with the Lord." (Page 29). Why would the Lord Almighty, maker of heaven and earth give divine revelation to a prophet that his pastor had just taken a shower? This kind of trivialization of prophecy does immense harm and causes confusion among the spiritually immature."[26]

The New Breed, Joel's Army

As I said earlier, one of Paul Cain's major messages seems to be that there is coming a new breed in the church, of overcomers. It is this company of end times people that the prophets have eagerly anticipated.

This army is also in the New Testament. It's referred to as "the manchild." I know some of you are going to disagree with this...Rev 12:25...Here it is this great army in the New Testament is the manchild. Rev 12:5, the overcomers Rev 2 and 3, the 144,000 servants, Rev 7:3, the bride or the lamb's wife, Rev 19:7 and 21:9, and the white horse, Rev 6:2, the first fruits, Rev 14:4, the precious fruits James 5:7, the wise virgins, Matt 25:1-13, the Manifested Sons of God, Rom 8:19-23 and it's certainly a remarkable fact that none of these names are expressions applied to the saints of God or at any other time in history. But all of them are in their context and promises showing undeniably that they belong to the end of time...To this present generation, Matt 24:34...and God wants us to realize once again in closing that there's going to be a great company of overcomers prepared for this mighty ministry which I call the prize of all the ages. And again, God's offering to the believers of this generation a greater privilege than was ever offered to any people of any generation at any time from ADAM clear down through the end of the millennium.[27]

Manifested Sons of God?

Rom 8:19 *For the earnest expectation of the creature waiteth for the manifestation of the sons of God.*

Unlike many others who espouse this doctrine, Paul Cain doesn't seem to balk at admitting to be a proponent of the Manifested Sons of God doctrine. The only problem that he seems to have with it is people trying to manifest their sonship presumptuously.

There will be a manifestation of the sons of God. And it won't be this baloney that we've heard of in the past; I mean there's been a few people tried to walk through a wall like this one over here and knocked their brain loose, but that's not what I'm talking about. I'm talking about a true manifested son of God; if anyone walks through this wall, over here, they're not going to tell you about it, I mean, they're just going to do it. And sons of God don't tell you they're sons of God, they'll just show you! Amen![28]

Romans 8:17 is the scriptural point at which the Manifested Sons of God proponents leap into error. The scripture teaches that the whole of creation indeed does await the time of manifestation of the sons of God, (ie the glorification of the saints, the final resurrection). The contention is that we believe we shall be glorified after the return of Jesus Christ bodily. It is then that He, Jesus, will put death underneath His feet. Manifested Sons of God teaches that there will be a company of supersaints who will be glorified and immortalized, before the bodily return of Jesus, and that we, the glorified, corporate Christ, will be the ones who put death under our feet. They also believe that only after that happens can Jesus return bodily. Clifford Hill summarizes it nicely in his **Prophecy Today** publication.

The opportunity of joining the "new breed" an elite group of believers endowed with supernatural power that would enable them to be a part of the army of dread warriors that God was said to be raising up in our generation. According to John Wimber this is a type of "Joel's Army" who will overcome all opposition to the gospel and eventually subdue the nations. This teaching is part of what is known as "dominion theology," which teaches that an elite army of overcomers will either destroy or subdue all the enemies of Christ until they eventually gain power and authority throughout the world. The government of the nations will be upon their shoulders and when all the secular authorities, governments, princes and kings have finally submitted to them, Christ will return and they will present the kingdom to Him.[29]

This is the theology that has been promoted by the Kansas City Prophets and their followers. As I have said earlier, it is a theology that emphasizes man in the place of Christ. The "corporate Christ" is still the church, not Christ. It is Jesus Christ who has destroyed death and will ultimately put it under His feet, we don't do it for Him.

The Challenge

In January, 1990, Ernie Gruen a Charismatic pastor in Kansas City for 27 years, of the Full Faith Church of Love, released a 233 page document listing erroneous prophecies, statements, doctrines, and incidents involving the Kansas City Prophets. "He accused KCF of sending out false prophets; of prophesying area churches to close down (and then join KCF) and of outright lying."[30]

As an example of the kind of "prophetic" response to these charges, here is an excerpt from Rick Joyner's **Morningstar**.

> KCF is just one of many new streams starting to flow in the body of Christ, each of which is destined to receive furious and unrelenting attacks for a season, much of which will come from those who may have a great influence on the church but have long ago lost the anointing.[31]

Do you see how the Berean spirit is being strangled here? When someone does raise some valid, specific criticism, "Well, it must be jealousy, they have a Saul spirit and don't like our 'David Movement.'" One of the most insidious and blinding concepts to come to the church lately is the idea that all criticism is personal. This idea is amplified by the emphasis on people who have the Jezebel Spirit, fault finding spirit, or that old standby, the accuser of the brethren! The whole idea deflects people's attention away from the issues of false, destructive doctrine and ministry to personality, "hurt," so called division and phony humility.

Gruen and Bickle were headed toward a resolution of their differences by a meeting of the Network of Christian Ministries, which was supposed to occur in July of 1990. But, in May, John Wimber stepped into the situation, offering himself and the Vineyard Movement as a "covering" to KCF and the prophets.

> Wimber acknowledged that there were indeed "excesses" at KCF. In a letter to Gruen, Wimber promised to address the errors and declared, "I am satisfied that we will not see these problems arising again in the future." The meeting with the NCM leaders was called off.[32]

Why? Didn't the errors still need to be examined, discussed, rejected or corrected? Shouldn't the Pentecostals at least have insisted on the opportunity to publicly, formally renounce these heresies? By sweeping the problem into the "Vineyard House" and not openly exposing and standing against it, we have sown the wind and are reaping the whirlwind! It was probably a great relief to everyone that Wimber's action saved us from another controversy, but what's the matter with controversy? Wimber did offer some correction and guidelines and it should be commended, but for the most part, the Kansas City Prophets rolled right along. The erroneous teachings were made available through the Vineyard Catalogues. Bob Jones was asked to "limit his public ministry," instead of being rejected from public or private ministry. John Paul Jackson (See our appendix of KCF Quotes), a blatantly false prophet was shipped out to California to minister there **with** Wimber. Paul Cain is widely accepted in England. Mike Bickle is a popular author, pastor and widely accepted Charismatic leader. Bickle, in looking back to 1990, told **Charisma** that he has learned four lessons from the experience.

1. "We had an elite spirit. That's become more and more real to me—it's so repulsive."
2. "We promoted mystical experience in a disproportionate way and it was disastrous."
3. "We were careless in the way we communicated prophetic words. This was hurtful in a lot of cases."
4. "We were wrong in the way we promoted the city church concept. I still believe in it, but now I believe it's a unity based on friendship."[33]

That's good, but weren't any of the prophecies, prophets, or mystical experiences blatantly false? What about false teaching? Do you still believe in the city wide church? Should Bob Jones have been renounced as a false prophet? There are still so many unresolved issues.

In all fairness, KCF and Vineyard Church did release a list of errors they had discovered and were correcting.

- Lack of accountability for prophecies that do not come true or do not bear witness to the person receiving the ministry.
- The attempt by some prophetic ministers to establish doctrine or practice by revelation alone, apart from clear biblical support.
- Dogmatic assertions in delivery of prophetic words.
- Revealing negative prophetic words in public without first confronting the individual.
- Giving prophetic words that affect a movement or church without going first to the appropriate levels of authority.
- The use of prophetic gifting for controlling purposes.
- Manifesting an attitude of superiority through the possession of a secret body of information. Amos 3:7 is true *surely the sovereign Lord does nothing without revealing His plan to His servants the prophets.* But the prophetic people are not to wear a garment of pride because of this knowledge.[34]

In 1991, Jones finally did have his messages pulled from the Vineyard Tape Catalog, after confessing to a moral failure. He is still cited as a credible prophet by many within the "prophetic movement," including many of those associated with the Toronto Blessing.

In conclusion, there is a severe judgement for following and supporting false prophets. I believe it was the acceptance and "covering" of these "prophets" that immediately accelerated this revival of spiritual drunkenness.

Jer 23:16 Thus saith the Lord of hosts, Hearken not unto the words of the prophets that prophesy unto you: they make you vain: they speak a vision of their own heart, and not out of the mouth of the Lord.

Ezekiel 13:1-9 And the word of the Lord came unto me, saying, Son of man, prophesy against the prophets of Israel that prophesy, and say thou unto them that prophesy out of their own hearts. Hear ye the word of the Lord; Thus said the Lord God; Woe unto the foolish prophets, that follow their own spirit, and have seen nothing! O Israel, thy prophets are like the foxes in the deserts. Ye have not gone up into the gaps, neither made up the hedge for the house of Israel to stand in the battle in the day of the Lord. They have seen vanity and lying divination, saying, The Lord saith: and the Lord hath not sent them: and they have made others to hope that they would confirm the word. Have ye not seen a vain vision, and have ye not spoke a lying divination, whereas ye say, The Lord saith it; albeit I have not spoken? Therefore thus saith the Lord God; Because ye have spoken vanity, and seen lies, therefore, behold, I am against you, saith the Lord God. And mine hand shall be upon the prophets that see vanity, and that divine lies: they shall not be in the assembly of my people, neither shall they be written in the writing of the house of the Israel, neither shall they enter into the land of Israel; and ye shall know that I am the Lord God.

End Notes

1. Audio Tape. "The Shepherd's Rod." Mike Bickle, Bob Jones. Fall, 1989.
2. Audio Tape Transcription. "Visions and Revelations." Mike Bickle and Bob Jones. Fall, 1989. Page 74.
3. Audio Tape. "The Prophetic History of Grace Ministries." Mike Bickle.
4. "Latter Day Prophets." Media Spotlight. Page 3. Al Dager.
5. Ibid.
6. "Resolving the Kansas City Prophets Controversy." Ministries Today. Lee Grady. Sept/Oct 1990.
7. "Latter Day Prophets."
8. "Visions and Revelations" Audio Tape Transcript. Page 60.
9. "Resolving the Kansas City Prophets Controversy."
10. "The Shepherd's Rod."
11. "What's the Problem?" Ernie Gruen.
12. "Resolving the Kansas City Prophets Controversy."
13. "Visions and Revelations."
14. Ibid.
15. Ibid.
16. Ibid.
17. Wes Campbell. October 14, 1994. Toronto Airport Vineyard.
18. "Grace City Report." December, 1989.
19. "Visions and Revelations."
20. Audio Tape, "The New Breed." Fall, 1989.
21. "Paul Cain: A Personal Profile." Terri Sullivant. "Grace City Report." Page 13.
22. Ibid.
23. Ibid.
24. Ibid.
25. "Latter Day Prophets." Media Spotlight, PO Box 290, Redmond, WA 98073-0290.
26. Clifford Hill. "Kansas City Prophets." Prophecy Today Magazine.
27. Audio Tape, Paul Cain. "Joel's Army." KCF's Southside Meeting.
28. "The New Breed."
29. Clifford Hill.
30. "Resolving the Kansas City Prophets Controversy."
31. Ibid.
32. Ibid.
33. "Kansas City Churches Reconciled." Charisma. Lee Grady. July, 1993.
34. "Making Corrections." Ministries Today. Sept/Oct, 1990.

7
The Roots: John Wimber and the Vineyard

The only accurate evaluation of any movement begins by looking at the roots. As it is written, *A good tree cannot produce evil fruit, nor can an evil tree produce good fruit.* Origin determines everything when it comes to spiritual evaluation. So many times we make our own judgments about things and get burnt! Eve looked at the fruit offered to her and said, basically, "It looks good to me!" Today many are looking at Toronto and saying "I know, it looks weird, but so much "good" is coming out of it. People are falling passionately in love with Jesus and Satan wouldn't want that!" Of course, there will be much apparent good to come from this movement! There has to be. How else would any Christians accept it? In this chapter we will take a step back into recent history and examine who is one of the main roots of the Toronto Blessing Phenomena; John Wimber and the Vineyard.

Who is John Wimber?

There are many conflicting opinions about the answer to that question. Some hail him as a "prophetic leader," and others as a "false prophet." He has certainly been a major influence on the church, during the last generation. First, as a gospel music writer, lecturer, author, pastor, evangelist, and builder of the Vineyard movement, John Wimber has worn many hats. Even before he was converted he was influential in the field of music, forming and managing the pop group, "The Righteous Brothers" and as a business man. By his own confession, in the early 1960s, as his music career soared, his marriage was diving, until 1962, which was the year that he was converted. Previously, he was despondent over being separated from his wife. Upon the advice of a friend, he went out into the desert to seek some peace, and cried out to God for help. When he got back to his hotel, a message from his wife awaited him telling him that she wanted to come back home. Both of them eventually began attending a Bible study group led by a Quaker, Gunner Payne, who became somewhat of a mentor to them, for a period, in the things of God. After six weeks of Bible study, John's wife, Carol, knelt down to accept Christ. Thirty seconds later, John found himself on the floor weeping, and calling on God. John left music, took a job at a factory and entered into discipleship. By 1970, he was the pastor of a Quaker church.

Wimber's wider scale influence on the body of Christ began in the mid 70s when he left the Quaker church to become the founder and lecturer for the Fuller Church Growth Institute. This travelling ministry gave him the opportunity to get a broad view of the church in America across denominational lines. He served more or less as a consultant to local churches on church growth and related issues and he became a highly sought after lecturer.

In this position, he came into contact with C. Peter Wagner, a fellow professor at Fuller and known as one of the leaders of the "church growth" movement. Wagner takes a very pragmatic approach to church growth. He has examined a wide spectrum of growing churches to find out "what is working" for them. In his book **Leading Your Church To Growth**, Wagner features everyone from the Southern Baptist Convention to Robert Schuller, from John Wimber to John MacArthur. This is very important for our understanding of Wimber, for he was greatly influenced by Wagner and vice versa. Wimber has developed a very pragmatic approach to ministry, healing, spiritual growth, etc. He has shown a willingness to examine and implement a wide range of what seems to be working in the Christian world, particularly in the area of healing.

Through his contact with Wagner, who for years was a missionary in Bolivia, as well as with other pastors and students from Third World countries, Wimber was exposed to the stories of supernatural confrontations, miracles, healings, demonic oppressions, and deliverances that are somewhat common in those places. He was also told of the explosive church growth wherever the power of God was demonstrated. This forced Wimber, who considered himself a cessationist (one who believes that miracles have ceased) to rethink his position. Three books that influenced him at this time were: **Concerning Spiritual Gifts**, by Donald Gee; **Healing and Christianity**, by Morton Kelsey; and **Look Out! The Pentecostals are Coming**, by C. Peter Wagner. Wimber, in the introduction to his book, **Power Evangelism**, assures us that he doesn't agree with all that Gee and Kelsey wrote, but they were used to cause him to reconsider the issue of spiritual gifts.

In 1977, Wimber left Fuller to put into practice the ideas he taught about evangelism and church growth, by starting a local church. That church began with a Bible study in his living room. It grew to 50 people and eventually swelled to some 6000 members and became known as the Vineyard Christian Fellowship of Anaheim, California. At first, they were affiliated with Chuck Smith's Calvary Chapels. Eventually, they disassociated and joined with another former Calvary group of seven churches, Ken Gullickson's Vineyard Fellowships. In the early 1980s Gullickson turned the leadership over to Wimber. Since then, there are approximately 600 Vineyard Churches worldwide.

A Watershed Event

In 1981 on Mother's Day, a service was held at the church Wimber pastored. This would prove to be significant enough to change Wimber's ministry. I believe that you will see striking similarities to the Toronto Blessing and other examples of mysticism we see today. The following account is narrated by Carol Wimber, John's wife.

On Mother's Day of 1981 we had a watershed experience that launched us into what today is called, "Power Evangelism." At this time, John [Wimber] invited a young man who had been attending our church to preach one Sunday evening. By now we had grown to over 700 participants. The young man shared his testimony, which was beautiful and stirring; then asked for all the people under the age of 25 to come forward. None of us had a clue as to what was going to happen. When they got to the front, the speaker said, "For years now, the Holy Spirit has been grieved by the church, but He's getting over it. Come, Holy Spirit." And He came. Most of the young people had grown up around our home. We had four children between the ages of 15-21. We knew the young people well. One fellow, Tim, started bouncing. His arms flung out and he fell over, but one of his hands accidentally hit a mike stand and he took it down with him. He was tangled up in the cord with the mike next to his mouth. The he began speaking in tongues, so the sound went throughout the gymnasium. We had never considered ourselves Charismatics, and certainly had never placed emphasis on the gift of tongues. We had seen a few people tremble and fall over before, and we had seen many healings. But this was different. The majority of the young people were shaking and falling over. At one point it looked like a battlefield scene, bodies everywhere, people weeping, wailing, speaking in tongues. And Tim in the middle of it all, babbling into the microphone. There was much shouting and loud behaviour!

John sat by quietly playing the piano and wide eyed! Members of our staff were fearful and angry. Several people got up and walked out...

But I knew God was visiting us. I was so thrilled because I had been praying for power for so long. This might not have been the way I wanted to see it come, but this was how God gave it to us...I asked one boy, who was on the floor, "What's happening to you right now?" He said, "It's like electricity. I can't move." I was amazed by the effect of God's power on the human body. I suppose I thought that it would be all inward work, such as conviction or repentance. I never imagined there would be strong physical manifestations.[1]

Now mind you, this was 1981 and yet note the striking parallels to the "Toronto Experience." Just on the surface, I can note several. For example:

1. It happened in a Vineyard Church
2. There was a prophecy in the name of the Holy Ghost
3. There was a prayer to the Holy Ghost
4. There were similar manifestations, bouncing, shaking, violently falling, weeping, electricity.

John Wimber was actually quite troubled by it all, until he received a sensual confirmation to the experience. I'll let Carol recount it:

John wasn't as happy as I. He had never seen large numbers of people sprawled out over the floor...He spent that night reading scripture and historical accounts of revival from the lives of people like Whitefield and Wesley...But his study did not yield the conclusive answers to questions raised from the previous evenings events. By 5 am, John was desperate, he cried out to God, "Lord, if this is you please tell me." A moment later the phone rang and a pastor friend of ours from Denver, Colorado was on the line. "John," he said, "I'm sorry I'm calling so early, but I have something really strange to tell you. I don't know what it means, but God wants me to say, "It's Me, John."[2]

Mystical Confirmation

Here also is a parallel with Toronto. For in their attempt to justify the mystical revival, scriptures are sought, mainly to interpret manifestations. Then church history is used extensively, citing anyone from George Fox to Teresa of Avila, to Jonathan Edwards, as though they belong together. Fox, founder of the Society of the Quakers, or Friends, taught that **every man** has an inward light that was sufficient in itself to lead him to know God. The Quakers took Fox's teaching to the point of elevating that subjective, inner witness above the objective Word of God. Teresa of Avila was a Roman Catholic mystic who had an almost complete spectrum of mystical experiences, out of body experiences, trances, and visitations of the Virgin Mary. And, of course, Jonathan Edwards, a late Puritan who wrote "Religious Affections" to defend the Great Awakening, a true revival based on the preaching of God's Word. All of these and others are thrown together to "defend" the Toronto Phenomena.

Notice in the above testimony, that Wimber didn't find any justification for what happened in church after spending a night in scripture. Nor did he in church history. It was only after a man in another city received a mystical confirmation that "It's Me," could John be assured that nothing was amiss. Ultimately with Toronto, it won't be scripture, or church history that confirms (Although there is a huge attempt to make Jonathan Edwards the theologian of their revival), rather it will be subjective experience, "I've gotten a new passionate love for Jesus now," "I felt God there," "An angel appeared to me," will be all the verification many will require, or, "I'm tired of not feeling God, this must be it!"

MC510, Signs, Wonders, and Church Growth

In the early 1980s, Wimber was invited to lecture at Fuller again. The course which he taught was entitled, "MC510, Signs, Wonders, and Church Growth." This course, which was immensely popular, was later renamed, "The Miraculous and Church Growth." It consisted of ten consecutive Monday evenings, for four hours each night. The first three hours consisted of a lecture, including questions, answers, and discussion. The last hour was a "lab" in which the gifts of the Spirit were demonstrated by Wimber and the class. Words of knowledge, healings, and deliverances were reported to have occurred, as Wimber and his students ministered one to another.

This course gained nationwide attention when Robert Walker, the editor of **Christian Life Magazine** devoted the October 1982 issue, now known as the "sold out" issue, to "Signs, Wonders, and Church Growth." That issue has since been reprinted as a book, **Signs and Wonders Today**, and according to C. Peter

Wagner, "It is currently being read as a study guide in churches and other Christian groups across the country."[3]

Many of the terms and concepts presented by the teaching have become common terminology since then. Terms like "Power Encounter," "Divine Appointment," "Power Evangelism," "Proclamation and Demonstration Evangelism," and "Paradigm Shift," are all being discussed, debated and commonly used today.

The essence of the "Signs and Wonders" teaching is this; there has been an explosive growth of Christianity in the Third World, while at the same time, it has stagnated in the developed, Western World. Why is this? At the risk of over simplification it is because the Gospel is being preached with kingdom power and demonstration in the Third World, and in the Western World, proclamation alone is the primary means of advancement. Church growth in the Third World is marked by the "Power Encounter," the ultimate confrontation between the Gospel witnesses and the entrenched Satanic opposition. (As in, Elijah and the Prophets and Baal). "Power Encounters" can be deliverances, miracles, healings, even "showdowns" with witch doctors, the clash between light and darkness, which ultimately brings the breakthrough in a given area.

Why is the Third World so much more open to God's kingdom power than the developed world? It is, according to Wimber, primarily because of world view. The Third World mentality is one in which Satan, demons, angels, elemental spirits, and even household gods, are interacting with us in everyday life. Those with this paradigm, or, world view, seem to have no problem with believing in a supernatural God or His miracles, in fact, they would expect God to perform miracles. Supposedly because their world view allows for this, it happens. With that kind of world view, God can be God!

But we in the Western World, have an entirely different mind set. We supposedly have what has been called a "two-tiered" mind. In the "upper story," we have God, Jesus, angels, and the supernatural. In the "lower story," we have everyday life, family, bills, responsibility, etc. And according to "Signs and Wonders" teaching, rarely do the two meet. In between the two compartments of our "paradigm" is what Wimber calls "the excluded middle," a layer of reality ignored by the Western world view. He describes this "excluded middle" in his "Signs and Wonders Church Growth" Syllabus this way:

Supernatural forces on this Earth includes
- spirits, ghosts, ancestors, demons
- earthly gods and goddesses who live within trees, rivers, hills, villages
- supernatural forces: maya, planetary influences, evil eyes, power of magic, sorcery, witchcraft
- Holy Spirit, angels, demons, signs and wonders, gifts of the Spirit[4]

This is supposedly the "layer of reality" that the Western world view has neglected, thus the call for a "Paradigm Shift," a radically new way of looking at reality! More on this important Wimber contribution to Toronto later.

The Third Wave

What made MC510 a novelty was that neither Wimber nor Fuller Seminary ever considered themselves even remotely Pentecostal or Charismatic. Therefore their teaching was acceptable to the thousands of evangelicals who were hungry for God and demonstrations of His power, but closed to anything associated with "tongues!" The idea was that the power of God is every bit as crucial to evangelism as the knowledge of God, and it is available to every believer. This would prove to be an idea whose time had come. (By the way, I do also believe that the gospel can and should be preached with confirming power according to Mark 16:9-10).

Those evangelicals who suddenly became aware of the power dimension of the Gospel, became known as "The Third Wave." According to C. Peter Wagner, "The First Wave was the Pentecostal movement, the Second, the Charismatics, and now the Third Wave is joining them."[5] The Third Wave being, of course, those mainstream evangelicals, now aware of the possibility of the power of God, but not wanting to identify with Pentecostalism.

There is no question that the Third Wave has significantly affected Christianity. A large number of our current leaders, authors, preachers, and scholars have been touched by it. I have already mentioned Robert Walker, and John Wimber, as well as C. Peter Wagner. Psychologist and popular Christian author, John White, (**Eros Defiled**, **The Golden Cow**, **The Fight**, and others), took a leave of absence from his practice in Canada and moved to Pasadena, California so that he and his wife could enroll in MC510, in 1981. He told C. Peter Wagner, "I had discovered I was trapped in what has been called a Western Mind set, a cultural bias that impeded my capacity to perceive the supernatural phenomena."[6] White wrote a book in 1988 called, **When the Spirit Comes With Power**, which is now being referred to as an explanation for some of the manifestations in Toronto. Much of the book amounts to a study of John Wimber and Vineyard and related manifestations.

Another man whom Wimber has influenced is Charles Kraft, Professor of Anthropology and Intercultural Communications at Fuller. He also spent time on the mission field in Nigeria, where he says he took a "powerless Christianity to Africa." According to Kraft,

As missionaries, we were well prepared in theological, cultural and linguistic studies. As evangelicals, however, we were totally unprepared to deal with the one area the Nigerians considered the most important—their relationships with the spirit world.[7]

His book, **Christianity with Power**, is a virtual testimonial to the influence of Wimber and the "Signs and Wonders" course, which he also took in 1982. But his book is much more than that. It is a call for a "Paradigm Shift," from a "Western Mind set" to a more experiential paradigm.

On the back cover of the book is the following headline and introductory paragraph:

What's Missing?

Power. Politicians crave it, money buys it, and some people will do anything for it.

In a world where New Agers rely on crystals and channelling to tap into spiritual power, the Christian is reminded that Jesus used supernatural power to heal the sick, cast out demons, and raise the dead. Two thousand years later, the world still desperately needs a Saviour who works in power. Charles Kraft believes that many modern Christians have become embarrassed and reluctant to preach a gospel accompanied by supernatural power. Our Western World view conditions us to fit God into a neat, predictable, mold.[8]

(Why blame it on world view? Whatever happened to unbelief?)

Don Williams is another author, theologian, professor and pastor who has been impacted by Wimber and the Third Wave. In his introduction to the book, **Signs, Wonders, and the Kingdom of God**, he makes the following acknowledgement.

A surprising turn in the road brought me into contact with John Wimber, the founder of The Vineyard Christian Fellowship, in Anaheim, California, in 1983. This led me into a whole new direction in ministry and a reformulation of its biblical basis. John became my pastor and friend for this current phase of my pilgrimage.[9]

Williams also counts Francis MacNutt among the major influences in his life.

There are so many others who have been directly or indirectly affected by Wimber and the Third Wave. Men like Ken Blue, Mike Bickle, Jack Deere, George Mallone, James Ryle, John Arnott, Randy Clark, and countless others. I think I have demonstrated to you where Wimber and Vineyard have come from, and the widespread influence on the church. I would emphasize that much of that influence has been positive, in my view. Bringing people into an awareness of the possibility of the demonstration of the Spirit and restoring a measure of the priesthood of every believer is a worthy accomplishment. Healing ministries have flourished in churches that used to be noted for not believing in healing, new churches have been planted, souls have been saved, compassion extended to the poor, all of this is good and I applaud it!

However, in my attempt to put Toronto in context, I will look now at four aspects of Wimber's contribution which I consider to be part of the problem. Toronto didn't happen "out of the blue," it is my contention that thousands have been pre-conditioned to enter into the mystical experiences that make up this revival. Here is what that conditioning has been composed of!

Paradigm Shift

Wimber, Kraft, White and Williams, as well as many other Third Wave teachers, have been calling for a "paradigm shift" for some time now. I have already outlined the teaching on "worldviews" and how they allegedly affect the demonstration of God's power. A paradigm shift is a total exchange of your world view! You once saw the gospel and the things of God through a certain grid; you now see it through an entirely different "grid!" I am beginning to think that thousands of Western Christians have "made the leap" into a new paradigm. This is the only way to explain the "Laughing Revival."

What is the shift? It is from a primarily Western, rational, logical, objective point of view to an Eastern, subjective, experiential paradigm. Haven't we been subtly taught over the years, that the Western mind set is cold, calculated, rational, based on just the observable facts? On the other hand, allegedly, the Eastern is mystical, from the heart, and based on experience?

Wimber teaches, "We must remember always that the Bible was written in the Middle East, not with rational assumption, that we bring to it as we try to understand it, but with an experiential assumption."[10] I interpret him to be saying that the Bible is not so much an objective book, but a subjective one. Not so much for understanding God mentally, but for experiencing Him intimately.

In another tape, Wimber explains: "You tell someone from the Far or Middle East that cotton only grows in warm semi-arid climates. England is cold and wet. [Ask them] Does cotton grow in England? The answer you'll get is, 'I don't know, I haven't been to England.'"[11] Or, "I can't say unless I've been there, (experience)." This is the new paradigm, a down playing of doctrine or "head knowledge" in favour of mystical experience. Another variation of this is, "God is bigger than His written word," translated, God wants to bring you into experiences that aren't in the limits of scripture. Just knowing God "doctrinally" is not sufficient, you now must have self authenticating experiences. All of these attitudes are the end result of the New Paradigm. This is the shift from primarily objective, to subjective thinking in our approach to truth!

Though there is so much lamenting about the "Western Mind set" that has "trapped" so many, we must ask ourselves two questions.

Is this a Biblical distinction?

Is this even a real problem? (ie Western *vs* Eastern Paradigm)

When Jesus was in His home town, the Bible says He could do no miracles there because of unbelief. These were Eastern people who certainly believed in God, angels, miracles, and had a Biblical world view. But when the Son of God came among them, He could do no miracles because of "unbelief." I don't think that unbelief is so much a cultural phenomena, as it is a moral one.

John 7:17 If any man do his will, he shall know of the doctrine, whether it be of God, or whether I speak of myself. (If you are willing to obey, you will be able to believe, not vice versa!)

*John 3:11-12 Verily, verily, I say unto thee, We speak that we do know, and testify that we have seen; and **ye receive not** our witness. If I have told you earthy things, and **ye believe not**, how shall ye believe, if I tell you of heavenly things?* (Notice, "You won't receive, or believe!")

Unbelief is a moral problem not an intellectual one.

Is trying to adapt a new cultural perspective Biblical? There is the renewing of the mind, but that is commanded of all, whether Eastern or Western.

Is it even real? Is someone with an Eastern Paradigm so dumb that they can't relate a simple problem in logic? (ie: cotton in England) I don't know, but I don't think so. I think that everywhere in the world there are people who are sensuous, and want to relate to God on primarily a sensual basis, feeling Him, visions, dreams, constant physical assurances. And also, everywhere in the world there are people who will be willing to take God at His Word, judging all things by the Word, willing to wait till the time when "We will be like Him for we will see Him as He is."

As I said, the new paradigm shift is one from a primarily objective knowledge of God with subjective experiences as a secondary aspect, to a primarily subjective view of God, with objective truth as secondary. In an audio cassette message called, "Healing, An Introduction," Wimber calls us to "know more personally the God who exists both beyond and within the boundaries of well defined doctrinal systems."[12] How can you really know God? Outside of doctrinal boundaries, right? Get out there beyond the doctrine, Eve! In another audio message, Wimber informs us, "All that is in the Bible is true, but not all truth is in the Bible. We integrate all truth, both Biblical and other into our experience of living."[13] It's the same old song and dance. "Don't be limited and narrow, we go beyond the scripture for truth, integrate it all into our 'experience.'" In the new paradigm, scripture is acknowledged and given lip service, but it is no longer the primary standard which measures spiritual reality. Subjective experience is now the center to which scripture must be measured. In short, "Have experience, will travel."

The Lowered Status of Scripture

In his book, **Power Evangelism**, Wimber explains, "God uses our experiences to show us more fully what He teaches us in scripture, many times toppling or altering elements of our theology and world view."[14]

As I explained earlier, experience now is ranked higher than doctrine, your doctrine can be toppled by your experience at times. What is doctrine or theology? Some nonessential detail? Is it negotiable? Biblical theology and doctrine are the body of truth. They are the only objective measure you have to test the spirits to see whether they be of God! We used to measure all experience by doctrine. In the new paradigm it is the doctrine that is suspect, and it is measured by degree of experience.

Wimber has consistently in his teaching pitted doctrine over against true experience, as if they were at variance! According to him, "God is greater than His Word."[15] As John Goodwin has said in his report on Vineyard, "As a result of this equating of experiential "truth" with the authority of scripture, Wimber's teachings are then validated by finding a Bible verse which appears as though it might apply to what has occurred."[16] The constant refrain about "dry Christians" who believe the right doctrine but don't know God from the heart, has a conditioning effect on God's people. "Because they believe the right doctrine and can give you the right answer doesn't mean they're born again."[17] OK, that's true, but what are you saying? Is there something wrong with Christians wanting to be doctrinally accurate? Here's another example: "That's what separates dead doctrine, from the living reality. There's a force of grace, there's a force of faith that must be manifest in our midst."[18] Don't just settle for more of that "dead doctrine," go after the impersonal force, right? Like Ken Copeland and others, evidently Wimber has accepted the occult idea of an impersonal force of faith and grace that must "manifest in our midst." Without this "force" energizing it, doctrine is supposedly dead. The truth is, all correct doctrine is living (Heb 4:12), the only dead doctrine is false doctrine.

John 6:63 It is the spirit that quickeneth; the flesh profiteth nothing: the words that I speak unto you, they are spirit, and they are life.

Heb 4:12 For the word of God is quick, and powerful, and sharper than any two-edged sword, piercing even to the dividing asunder of soul and spirit, and of the joints and marrow, and is a discerner of the thoughts and intents of the heart.

I wonder about the teacher who lashes out at sound doctrine, and would make a distinction between the Word of God taught and "living reality." In his teaching on Luke 5:18-24, Wimber accuses fundamentalists of "chiselling" at ministry, with the Word!

Many of you and myself included, have committed that sin. We have been theologically correct as we've attempted to conform something to scripture, saying, "At this point the teaching is..." Many fundamentalists do exactly the same thing today about the works of the Spirit. They take the Word of God and chisel at a practice or a ministry or a flow, without recognizing it's God moving. Not recognizing that God is bigger than His written Word.[19]

As John Goodwin points out, the affect of this kind of teaching is to identify "Those who measure a practice or ministry by scripture with the unbelieving scribes."[20] Incredibly, in the same teaching, he pits doctrine against the work of the Spirit!

Jesus, knowing their hearts, said, "Why are you thinking evil in your heart?"...I said, "Lord they're not thinking evil...they're just operating under sound doctrine"...But you see, it's evil when you don't recognize God. It's evil when you don't see Jesus in the things that are going on. It's evil when you hide behind doctrinal beliefs that curtail and control the work of the Spirit...The church today is committing evil in the name of sound doctrine. And, they are quenching the work of the Holy Spirit. And they are turning against the work of the Holy Spirit.[21]

Evidently, Wimber stands on the side of the "Work of the Spirit," but those who would dare appeal to scriptural confirmation are trying to curtail and control the work of the Spirit, hiding behind doctrinal beliefs.

Mysticism

Another Wimber contribution, reflected in Toronto, is mysticism. What is mysticism? Mysticism is the sensualization of our relationship with God and dealings with the spirit realm. By sensualizing, I am not referring to sexuality, but with the feeling realm. A mystic is someone who wants to know God intimately, but is not patiently waiting for the "beatific vision." He wants to see, touch, feel, and be one with God **NOW**. The mystic asks, Why can't we feel God? See Him? Go deeper and deeper with Him, into deeper levels of intimacy? We can, but in His time and on His terms.

I Cor 13:12-13 For now we see through a glass darkly; but then face to face: now I know in part; but then shall I know even as also I am known. And now abideth faith, hope, and charity, these three; but the greatest of these is charity.

I Cor 15:49-53 And as we have borne the image of the earthy, we shall also bear the image of the heavenly. Now this I say, brethren, that flesh and blood cannot inherit the kingdom of God; neither doth corruption inherit incorruption. Behold, I shew you a mystery; We shall not all sleep, but we shall all be changed, In a moment, in the twinkling of an eye, at the last trump: for the trumpet shall sound, and the dead shall be raised incorruptible, and we shall be changed. For this corruptible must put on incorruption, and this mortal must put on immortality.

I John 3:1-2 Behold, what manner of love the Father hath bestowed upon us, that we should be called the sons of God: therefore the world knoweth us not, because it knew him not. Beloved, now are we the sons of God, and it doth not yet appear what we shall be: but we know that, when He shall appear, we shall be like him; for we shall see him as he is.

The mystic does not accept the fact that our salvation is not yet complete. The hunger "to know and be known" is good, but coupled with the discontented impatience, and a low or distorted view of scripture, and you have a mystic.

Toronto is a mystical revival. The work of the Spirit is relegated to the level of sensual manifestation. People are trying to feel God and they have tapped into something.

In his Healing Seminar Syllabus, Wimber has taught thousands different healing techniques. In teaching them to recognize the anointing that ministers healings, they are to look for "sensations of warmth (flowing out of hands), [Aura manipulation], tingling feelings, trembling of hands, and a sense of anointing."[22] Allegedly, "These spiritual phenomena are manifestations of the Spirit's presence on the person. By observing them you can begin to see what the Spirit is doing in and through the person. We don't have an explanation for all the various manifestations."[23]

Not having an explanation for these manifestations doesn't discourage him though, for,

Sometimes you can learn more from what's not said than what's said, [in scripture]. If you take today's practices and put it up against the scripture, lots of stuff falls off, there's no place to put it.[24]

Lack of Use of Discernment

Toward the mid to late 1980s, Wimber became enamoured by the ministry team of the Kansas City Fellowship, or "The Kansas City Prophets." At an August 1989 conference in Denver, Colorado, Wimber called on Vineyard pastors to receive their ministry.

I think you'll find that the prophets are pretty nice people by and large, I've come to know several of them here, I think maybe five or six, that are from Kansas City Fellowship. And then we have Paul Cain, that lives in Dallas and has had quite a relationship with Kansas City for a number of years, but is not evidently technically considered a Kansas City Prophet. You'll hear from them, some this week, although they won't be largely behind the scenes. They've already ministered significantly this weekend. And, it's my hope that every one of you, if you've not today had the occasion of sitting down with one or two of them and having them minister to you, that that will happen before the week is over. Because I believe that in God's providence you'll be blessed and you'll go home with your pockets full and you're heart singing, if they do so. [25]

Interestingly enough, in 1990, when the Kansas City Prophets began to be exposed as fraudulent, it was to Wimber that they went for "correction." But he never stopped promoting the erroneous teachings of Paul Cain, Mike Bickle, Bob Jones, John Paul Jackson. In 1991, he did stop promoting Bob Jones, but not because of heresy, but because of immorality.

The point is that Wimber, by his acceptance of false prophets, has paved the way for an unquestioning acceptance of "prophets." I'm all for modern day prophets as long as they will submit to the tests of Deut 18 and Deut 13. But these prophets actually boasted about the margin of error that the Lord had graciously allowed! They believe that prophets today have to learn, so they start out at a small percentage of accuracy and "grow" in their gifting. This is the same claim that psychics make!

Another area of lack of discernment is in the techniques of healing, which Wimber has promoted. They are highly syncretistic and also highly mystical. His syncretistic approach to healing can be seen in his books, tapes, and seminars. In them he includes as equally valid: inner healing, healing of memories, modern psychology, self forgiveness, visualization, the teachings of Francis MacNutt, Matthew and Dennis Linn, John and Paula Sandford, etc. In his video series, "Healing," tape one, Wimber teaches us what to look for in healing.

Hot flushes and stiffness in certain parts of the body, tingling sensations, trembling and shaking, falling down under the power of the Spirit, strong electrical currents, ripples on the skin, movement under the skin, radiance on the face, heavy breathing, moaning, groaning, and falling into a trance.[26]

It's this combination of sensual confirmation and non-discernment that has conditioned a whole generation to seek mystical experiences, which are evidently being granted to them in Toronto and other places.

Listening to this incredible view of the scene in Luke 4:40-41 brings Toronto to mind,

See the crowd dynamics? They brought people to him, they brought people to him, they brought people to him. What's happening on Sunday night at our church? They're bringing people, they're bringing people...This wasn't a neat crowd. There were probably people flipping and flopping all over the ground, manifesting demons...People with foam running down their faces who had just barfed all over themselves. They were screeching like animals. They were bringing people with chains on them that were tied. This is frenzy, people. This is not calm, this is not orderly. This is frenzy, this is frantic.[27]

Go into a meeting full of people who have that interpretation of the Bible and watch what happens!

John MacArthur writes in a recent book,

An appendix in Wimber's Power Evangelism, seeks to establish that signs and wonders have appeared throughout church history. Wimber cites an eclectic catalogue of individuals and movements—both orthodox and heretical—as evidence. Included in these are Hilarion (a fourth century hermit), Augustine, Pope Gregory I (The Great), Francis of Assisi, The Waldenes (who opposed the Pope and were persecuted by the Dominicans), Vincent Ferrer (who was himself a Dominican), Martin Luther, Ignatius Loyola (founder of the Jesuits), John Wesley, and the Jansenists (a Catholic sect). In a booklet published by The Vineyard, Wimber adds The Shakers (a cult that demanded celibacy), Edward Irving (discredited leader of the Irvingite sect in 19th century England), and the supposed miracles and healings worked by an apparition of the Virgin Mary at Lourdes, France![28]

In another teaching tape on the subject of healing, Wimber advises,

In the Catholic Church for over a 1,200 year period people were healed as a result of touching the relics of the saints. We Protestants have difficulty with that...but we healers shouldn't because there's nothing theologically out of line with that.[29]

In Conclusion

We have to remember that the things happening in Toronto, are happening in a Vineyard context. Therefore, the contribution of John Wimber has to be looked at. Praise God for bringing "signs and wonders attending the Word" to the church's attention. However, the conditioning of God's people in four areas in particular, has set the stage for the "Mystical Revival." These are:

• Paradigm Shift - The call for a new world view, a shift from an objective approach to God's truth, to an almost entirely experiential approach. To attempt to abandon your entire world view, particularly, your "Western rationalistic paradigm," and replace it with a more subjective view, leaves a person open for seduction.

• The Denigration of Doctrine and Theology - The constant down playing of the "head knowledge and theology" which is the teaching of the Bible. Partially because of this kind of influence, it is the one who insists on measuring all things spiritual by the scripture, who is now suspect, as a narrow minded scribe or Pharisee! The only "sin" now recognized is the "sin" of critical thinking.

• Thirdly, the blatant mysticism. Wimber has taught people to look for the anointing, the "force of faith and grace," the power to heal, and the activity of God through physical sensations. A whole group of Christians are now aware of "tingling," "radiant glow," expecting to tremble, feel electricity, and a host of other manifestations that have been catalogued.

• Finally, the confusion of Wimber's syncretistic approach. Almost every approach is equally valid, from laying on of the believer's hands, to Roman Catholic relics. To him, George Fox, Jonathan Edwards, Teresa of Avila, and Ignatius of Loyola all belong in the same category! This has sown much confusion into the church.

All the groundwork has been laid (unwittingly) for the Mystical Revival. All that was needed was a bold, innovative, Charismatic catalyst. One came to this country from South Africa in 1987...Rodney Howard Browne.

End Notes

1. "Carol Wimber, A Hunger for God." Kevin Springer, ed. Power Encounters. Harper and Row. 1988.

2. Ibid.

3. C. Peter Wagner. "The Third Wave of the Holy Spirit." Vine Books. Page 25.

4. J. Wimber. "Signs, Wonders, and Church Growth" Section 3, "Today's Tension with the Miraculous: World View" Vineyard Ministries International. Placentia, California.

5. Wagner, 13.

6. John White quoted in Wagner, 29.

7. Charles Kraft. "Christianity With Power." Vine Books. Pages 3-4.

8. Ibid. Back Cover.

9. Don Williams. "Signs, Wonders, and the Kingdom of God." Vine Books.

10. F.V. Scott. "John Wimber and the Vineyard Ministries" Page 19.

11. J. Wimber. "Ministering in England." Audio Tape (Media Spotlight Report). John Goodwin "Testing the Fruit of the Vineyard."

12. J. Wimber. "Healing, An Introduction." Audio Tape #5. Vineyard Ministries Inc. 1985.

13. J. Wimber. "Vineyard 83 Leadership Conference, The Five Year Plan."

14. J. Wimber. "Power Evangelism." Harper and Row. 1986. Page 89.

15. J. Wimber. "Church Planting Seminar." Audio Tape, 5 volume. 1981.

16. John Goodwin. "Testing the Fruit of the Vineyard." Al Dager's Media Spotlight Special Report. Goodwin was a Vineyard pastor for eight years and travelled extensively with Wimber.

17. J. Wimber. Healing Seminar Series.

18. Ibid.

19. Ibid.

20. Goodwin. "Testing the Fruit of the Vineyard."

21. Wimber. Healing Seminar Series.

22. Wimber. Healing Seminar Syllabus II Observations A. Spiritual Phenomena. Pages 74-75.

23. Wimber. Healing Seminar Series.

24. Wimber. Healing Seminar Series.

25. J. Wimber. "Unpacking Your Bags." Undated audio tape.

26. J. Wimber. 1985 Healing Video Series. Tape 1 VMI. Placentia, California.

27. Wimber. Healing Seminar Series.

28. John MacArthur, Jr. "Charismatic Chaos." Zondervan Books. Page 180.

29. J. Wimber. Healing Seminar. Three tapes. 1981. Tape #1.

8
Rodney Howard Browne

Two Contrasting Experiences

He walked with Jesus for three years. He had even been in the inner circle of the three closest friends of Jesus. It was he who had first received the revelation that Jesus is the Christ, the son of the Blessed One. Sure, there had been many rough times as well. Walking with Jesus as a disciple had subjected him to countless rebukes and corrections. With Jesus, the rebuke of instruction was a way of life. But there had been so many glorious experiences. Like the time they went up on the holy mountain, and had seen the true glory of Jesus revealed, in the transfiguration, the cloud of God had overshadowed them, Moses and Elijah had appeared and they heard a discussion between Jesus, Moses and Elijah! On the way back down the mountain, Jesus patiently answered the questions that the three peppered Him with and then cautioned them to tell no one the experience until He was raised from the dead. And recently, Peter had an even more ultimate experience, he had seen and talked with the resurrected and glorified, Lord Jesus Christ! As he stood up to testify, that Pentecost Sunday morning, he looked out at the crowd which had gathered and with a boldness he had previously never known, preached the significance of the recent events with clarity, and conviction from the Psalms and the book of Joel. He made known to that crowd, that "this Jesus, whom you crucified, God has raised up." The crowd was pierced through with conviction and shouted, "What shall we do?" Peter led 3000 to the Lord that day.

An Even Stronger Experience?

He had gone to about 100 of his brother's evangelistic meetings, but so far had been "untouched," at least not in the way that thousands of others had been. Hundreds of others were struck dumb, paralysed, intoxicated, unable to do anything but laugh or weep and moan. Then it happened. An angel walked up to him and touched his stomach. He went down "under the power." The next thing he saw was the angel pouring out of a vase, what looked like honey, on him. The more the angel poured, the drunker he got.

When he stood up at a subsequent meeting to testify, his brother asked him,

"Basil, tell the people what happened to you." [Basil], "Um, well, um...[heavy breathing]...We were...we were...um..." [Basil is standing there, with glazed eyes, half stooped, locked in a hunched position, totally out of it.]

[Rodney Howard Browne] "And then what happened?" [crowd laughter]

[Basil] "Umm, and then I, umm, ooh, hmmm, [out of breath] OOOH, Whew! Whew! MMMM, Heh, and....ummm."

[Rodney Howard Browne] "The fire..." [interestingly, at this point, Basil is sweating and turning red, physically hot, which is somewhat common in this renewal].

[Basil] "OOOH! Oh, whew, and um, then..."[heavier breathing and groaning][1]

At this point, Rodney calls the ushers forward to help him to his seat. The crowd is absolutely delighted. Another confirmation of the ministry of Rodney Howard Browne!

Could this be an even stronger experience than Peter had? Peter had only walked with Jesus three years, been with Him at the mount of transfiguration, and witnessed the resurrected Christ. But he could testify intelligently about it later! The experiences that Basil had, were supposedly so strong, so sacred and so dynamic, he couldn't even testify about them in intelligent speech! He almost appeared to go into a catatonic state, or a trance when asked to testify. He also exhibited semi-paralysis and appeared to be extremely hot, and turning red, sweating as he spoke of the fire. Welcome to the ministry of Rodney Howard Browne!

The whole testimony service recorded by video July 21, 1994, is unbelievable! The video was actually given to me to commend the ministry of Rodney Howard Browne! The fruit of this ministry was prominently displayed. People were standing there and going into trances, unable to speak intelligibly. They were so far out of it you'd think they were on Valium. What are they testifying of? Was it the cross? Was it Jesus? Their testimony was of their recent mystical experience, and how it has changed their lives. It is quite certain that the mystical experience that Rodney Howard Browne and others are initiating people into, actually does change lives. This "revival" is the forerunner of a massive change for many lives. Be aware that this is not a change akin to the transforming power of the gospel! The change that is being introduced here is not wrought by truth, gradually adapted and conformed to, this change is solely experiential. This is the paradigm shift that has been called for, Christians have finally "turned off their heads" so that they can actually experience "God" for once, instead of just having "head knowledge."

Rodney's Family Touched

Not only his brother, but his mother and wife testified. Rodney assures us on the tape, if your family gets it, it's real. When Andronica, his wife, testified, she gave one of those, "I've always considered myself to be dignified, but God wanted to break me out of it," testimonies. According to her, when the "holy laughter" phenomena first broke out, disrupting services and interrupting preaching, she was somewhat put off. She would almost cringe whenever her husband would say to the people, "I command you to laugh." But she eventually got to the point where she was able to "let go". As she told Bob and Molly DeAndrea on the "Good Life" Christian television show, "Because I let go, I felt a bubbling come up from my belly. I started to analyze it, but I heard the Lord say, 'Don't think, just let me do it.'" Andronica has been changed! She says she no longer cares what people think, it doesn't even bother her when people don't go along with the laughter, "The people sitting there with serious faces are the funniest ones."

Next up to testify after Andronica, was Rodney's mom. "Mom tell the people what happened to you." [Mother] "Well...um...and he...then I...um, you see..." This is literally how it went for about five minutes. She had come into some experience so powerful, she was unable to testify of it in intelligent sentences! Even the apostles never had such a marvellous encounter with God. After trying to talk about it, she just began laughing, shouting, dancing and praising God before falling under the power. After leading her to her seat, Rodney Howard Browne tells a delighted audience, "She hasn't been able to tell me what happened yet..."

Janny Grien and Others

The testimony service just kept getting worse, (or better, depending on your perspective). Janny Grien, internationally known gospel songwriter and singer, was called up. She too was asked to testify, (not to Jesus, but to her "mystical experience"). She literally puffed and sputtered, pulled at her collar, got red and hot, breathed heavy and couldn't speak intelligibly trying to relate this "miraculous experience." She did come to enough to say something to the effect of "I was fine till I came up here [to the stage]," eventually. She ultimately "went down" under the power. Another pastor was called up, with a blank look on his face, obviously in a trance, he shuffled to the mike. When asked for his testimony, he stared blankly at the audience, unable to say anything, except an extremely slurred "Praise God." He had to be helped back to his seat. Rodney Lloyd, Bible school teacher, could do a little better. He, at least, could talk somewhat sensibly. He told us of his experience, going down under the power at a Rodney Howard Browne meeting and how God verified the validity of this meeting by levitating his arm!

Who Is Rodney Howard Browne?

He was born into a Pentecostal home, an atmosphere that was bathed in prayer. By his own testimony, he was saved at the age of five and baptized in the Holy Spirit at age eight. Both at home and in the Pentecostal church he attended, he testifies of "continually [seeing] supernatural manifestations."[2]

His own "baptism of fire" occurred in 1979, while he was still a teenager. Here is how he tells it.

I knew that there was more, much more...In July of 1979, I cried out to God in sheer desperation. I wanted Him to manifest Himself to me and in me. I was hungry...As I prayed that day, I told the Lord, "Either you come down here and touch me, or I am going to come up there and touch you." I was desperate. I must have called out to God for about 20 minutes that day. Suddenly, the fire of God fell on me. It started on my head and went right down to my feet. His power burned in my body and stayed like that for three whole days...I was really praying, "Lord, I am too young to die." In the fourth day, I am not praying, "O Lord send your glory," I am praying, "Please lift it off me so that I can bear it." I was plugged into heaven's electric light supply...my desire has been to go and plug other people in. My whole body was on fire...Out of my belly began to flow a river of living water. I began to laugh uncontrollably and then I began to weep and then speak with tongues. I was so intoxicated on the wine of the Holy Ghost that I was beside myself...Because of that encounter with the Lord, my life was radically changed from that day on.[3]

Rodney Howard Browne proceeds in the book to relate changes in his ministry after that anointing with fire, while preaching in a Methodist church. I'll let him tell it in his own humorous way.

We were preaching in a Methodist church. I was back in the vestibule—which is a holy name for a plain old office—preparing for service. One of the young ladies came into the office and asked me to pray for her because she was in terrible pain...I got my hand halfway to her head, almost like a gunslinger would draw a gun out of a holster, and point it at his opponent. Suddenly, unexpectedly, it felt like my finger tips came off. I felt a full volume of anointing flow out of my hand. The only way I can explain it is to liken it to a fireman holding a fire hose with a full volume of water flowing out of it. The anointing went right into her. It looked like someone had hit her in the head with an invisible baseball bat and she fell to the floor...[4]

On and on it goes.

Notice the sensuality of the testimony, though. The fire of God courses through his body, it shoots out of his fingers, like a gun, she gets hit by an invisible bat! The concept behind the word sensual is not always referring to "sexual." Sensual refers to the things pertaining to the five physical senses. Rodney Howard Browne has a very sensual ministry. The promise is held out that you are going to be touched by God, you're going to feel God, you'll even get drunk on the new wine! You'll laugh, stagger, get stuck to the floor, and generally have an all out good time! It's "fun" going to these meetings!

Back to Who is Rodney Howard Browne?

In 1987, Rodney Howard Browne left his native South Africa to come to the United States, on a "word from God." By that time, he had already pioneered a church, pastored for a time and been on the pastoral staff of Ray McCauley's Rhema Bible Church in Johannesburg. Upon arriving in America, he commenced an itinerant ministry.

It was at a series of meetings in Albany, New York in 1989 that the unusual manifestations had begun to take place. It began to occur at a time when both he and his wife were hungry for God to move. As he was preaching at a morning meeting, he said a cloud filled the room, visible to others, but not to him. He could feel it, though. People began falling out of their seats as he preached.

> While I was preaching, the power of God began to fall. Many people began to fall out of their seats. It looked like someone was shooting them and in some places whole rows at a time would go down. They were laughing and crying and falling all over the place and looked like drunken people.[5]

Rodney Howard Browne became an internationally prominent revivalist after a Spring, 1993 meeting at an Assembly of God church in Lakeland, Florida, the Carpenter's Home Church. He was scheduled for one week, but the meeting lasted four! People who heard about it flew in from as far away as Africa, Great Britain and Argentina. What made the difference in this revival meeting? According to **Charisma Magazine**,

> The difference was the laughter. No matter what Howard Browne did or said, hundreds who attended the daily sessions always ended up on the sanctuary floor in helpless laughter. When the services were broadcast on radio, more curious seekers showed up to join the fun.[6]

An Incredible Interview

One of those who heard Rodney Howard Browne services on the radio was Molly DeAndrea. Along with her husband, Bob, the DeAndrea's host a local Christian television show, "The Good Life." On one of their shows, they interviewed both Rodney and Andronica Howard Browne. In the interview, Molly DeAndrea testified of listening to one of the services on the radio at home. At one point, she tried to get up to go to the bathroom and was "stuck," immobilized and had to stand there in one position for one hour and ten minutes, laughing helplessly. As she stood there, she testified of her feet being on fire, so hot that she became afraid that they were going to be blistered! "You know it's the presence of God" she assures us.

The interview was interspersed with various clips of Rodney's meetings. For example:

[You hear] [Rodney Howard Browne] "Welcome to Joel's Place—have another drink. You can have a double of what he's having."

[Rodney Howard Browne] "Does your mother know you're here? Where are you from, sir?" [answer unheard]

[Rodney Howard Browne] "I command you to laugh."

[Obviously intoxicated young man] "I came here tonight and I was going to get high on both spirits—I'm about half drunk right now—but everybody's laughing and falling on the floor and I want some of that."

[Rodney Howard Browne] "You do? You have to be willing to come to God."

[Young Man] "If you give me some of that, I want to come back." [Crowd applauds wildly as young man "accepts Jesus" and is slain "in the Spirit."]

Interview Highlights

This particular interview did a great job of presenting to the public who Rodney Howard Browne actually is and what he stands for. The different manifestations were discussed, such as "the heat." By the heat, I mean an actual sensation of the fire, people are feeling heat, their faces are turning red, and they feel that it is God's glory. [Rodney Howard Browne] "It's like putting a finger into a light socket, it's tangible and real." As I said earlier, as soon as Rodney Howard Browne mentioned "the fire" to his brother Basil, he visibly got hot and sweaty.

Another manifestation that was discussed on the show was the strange physical positions people end up in, whenever this particular spirit moves. Andronica tells of people weeping and laughing and rolling on the floor laughing hilariously, unable to stop and then adds, "When those waves of anointing hit you, you can't do anything else." We are also told that, "You know it's not hype because tough guys, determined not to fall down do anyway." A clip is shown of someone who was struck dumb, known only as Stacy's wife.

[Stacy's Wife] "We were in Spring Hill and..." [laughter of people]
[Rodney Howard Browne] "And then what happened?"
[Stacy's Wife] "...[long pause, troubled breathing, clearing throat]..."
[Rodney Howard Browne] "So holy, God is so holy, He's such a holy God."

It's not unusual to have bodies immobilized, people struck dumb, there have been people acting like they are swimming in the River of Life, as they are "laid out." People "flying" like eagles around the room and others seen running in place. People get stuck to the floor all the time, much to the delight of the thoroughly entertained crowds. "Religious people will not understand this..."

Buddhist for 25 Years

[Rodney Howard Browne] "There are unusual things that happen, it doesn't happen in every church."

[Host] "One man in Spring Hill, I remember, he came in as an unbeliever and very sceptical and then he testified...two days later, how the Lord just kind of put this heavy load on him and stuck him to the floor, and then his head was stuck to the floor."

[Rodney Howard Browne] "Now he was a Buddhist for 25 years and God had saved him and he come into the meeting and said, "These people are just wacko" ...The power of God hit him cause he said, 'Lord, you haven't proven anything to me,' and God hit him in the seat and he crumbled and he doubled over and his head got down to where his feet were and he ended up with his rear right up in the air, and he was stuck like that and he couldn't move...when he got up off the floor, he knew that God's power had touched him. Now some would say, "I don't believe it." That's fine, those people that don't want to believe it they probably wouldn't believe nothing. They probably wouldn't believe the Bible."

Another topic discussed was "religious people" or the church in general. Rodney Howard Browne never seems to miss a chance to berate and mock those who are hesitant about this "move of the Spirit." That should be a warning to many, but all too often instead, it actually intimidates the ones who should be sounding the alarm.

[Rodney Howard Browne] "Those who don't believe this probably wouldn't believe anything, they probably wouldn't believe the Bible." Andronica parrots a host of other voices when she proclaims, "Some people have more faith that the devil will show up than the Holy Spirit!" Rodney doesn't even bat an eye when he accuses the church of taking the supernatural out of the Bible and making it into **Readers Digest** or an encyclopedia. Does the church need this? [Rodney Howard Browne] "The church needs laughter, Lord have mercy! [They're] the driest bunch on the planet." Also, "The religious dead heads have left and some dead preachers, but the unsaved and backsliders are here."

Is It Scriptural

Rodney does attempt to answer this question with proof texts. Is it scriptural for laughter to interrupt the preaching of the Word? Acts chapter 10, *While he yet spake, the Holy Ghost fell...for they heard them speak with tongues.* What about trances? Peter went into a trance in Acts 10. Spiritual drunkenness is supposedly taught in Acts 2 and Eph 5:18, Ps 126 is used to support uncontrollable laughter, Zechariah was struck dumb in Luke chapter 1. In Acts chapter 8:1, the Samaritans received the Word with joy. I Corinthians 2:4-5 tells us of demonstrations of the Spirit, are you beginning to see what I mean? Of course, there will be chapter and verse used to back up everything being said and done. But the ultimate question is, did Jesus or the apostles ever even remotely utilize these practices? (Also uses I Cor 2:14, Acts 9, etc.)

What's it like to be in the influence of this "spirit?" [Rodney Howard Browne] "The ladies enter in easier than men, for they have had to learn to submit." (Eve entered so much quicker than Adam.)

[Molly DeAndrea] "Sometimes you can think and can't talk, other times you're blank—you can't think, you clear your throat like you're getting ready to do something, but can't do anything."

[Rodney Howard Browne] "What happens is, the power of God overwhelms people to such a place that it's very hard to function. In the natural, people don't understand. We have a spirit man and we live in a physical body. Well, when the glory of God comes on you and overwhelms you, you can think exactly what you're going to say...but you are so over in the spirit, you are so lost in the spirit, it's very hard to function...You can't make that up and you wouldn't want to..."

The Teachings of Rodney Howard Browne

Rodney doesn't want anyone to get upset by the possibility of anyone getting "in the flesh" at one of these meetings. In one of his books, he explains it this way,

> You can't have revival without stirring up the flesh. If you want to stop the flesh, you'd better shoot everyone as they come in the door. How can you stop the flesh from manifesting in the house of God, when it is manifesting continually in the world?...When revival comes you will see manifestations of these three things in meetings: (1) the Holy Spirit; (2) the flesh, and (3) the devil. But I'd rather be in a church where the devil and the flesh are manifesting than in a church where nothing is happening because people are too afraid to manifest anything...Don't worry about it. And if a devil manifests, don't worry about that, either. Rejoice, because at least something is happening![7]

I think these comments reflect the growing kind of discontent, that paves the way for the mystical revival. The discontent is basically summed up by the above statement, in effect, "I don't care if it's flesh, Holy Spirit or the devil, just let something happen!"

Howard-Browne's view of recent church history is revealing as well. In his book, **The Coming Revival**, Browne praises William Branham as a great man of God, and the Latter Rain Movement as a valid move of the Spirit. In this book, he councils us to "ride the wave," making sure you "read the wave" to make sure it's a "right wave" as opposed to a "wrong wave." As soon as the "wave is over, look for the next wave, and when that wave is over look for the next."[8] He doesn't explain how to "read" waves, though.

This kind of thinking is the very antithesis of the admonition Paul gave us in Ephesians chapter 4, where he told us that we should mature in Christ so that, *We will no longer be infants tossed back and forth by the waves and blown here and there by every wind of doctrine and by the cunning craftiness of men whereby they lie in wait to deceive.* James equates waves as those things which toss the double minded, unstable person to and fro.

James 1:5-8 If any of you lack wisdom, let him ask of God, that giveth to all men liberally, and upbraideth not; and it shall be given him. But let him ask in faith, nothing wavering. For he that wavereth is like a wave of the sea driven with the wind and tossed. For let not that man think that he shall receive any thing of the Lord. A double minded man is unstable in all his ways.

The Vineyard Movement also consider themselves to be a wave, "The Third Wave," (The first being the Pentecostal Revival, the second the Charismatic Movement). Many I interviewed in Toronto expressed gratitude that they had jumped on this particular "wave." In a recent editorial in **Charisma Magazine**, the concept of the wave is redefined, into a potentially positive phenomena, after quoting *Ephesians 4:14 That we henceforth be no more children, tossed to and fro, and carried about with every wind of doctrine, by the sleight of men, and cunning craftiness, whereby they lie in wait to deceive.* The author expressed a peculiar "insight" into this verse.

It's important to note that Paul did not specify whether these winds of doctrine were true or false teachings. [?] Indeed, dogma does not have to be false to be misleading. Even a true doctrine with an overly exaggerated emphasis can sidetrack us from Christlikeness.

You've got to watch out for true doctrine now, it can throw you off. The author goes on to say in his article that,

In the passage in Ephesians, Paul also says that our pursuit of Christlikeness keeps us from being "tossed here and there by waves" (v 14). A wave is a spiritual phenomena that sweeps over a church or city—a spiritual high tide in which we can be washed and healed. A true spiritual wave can release wonderful joy and bring healing to areas within us otherwise untouched by God.[9]

There you have it, a wave is a desirable thing, or as the author of the article goes on to say, "an act of grace." It is true that the author's purpose seems to be to caution people not to get hung up on the comings and goings of the waves, but rather to reach for conformity to Christ. But the point I make in this, is that waves are now considered to be good things, and people are being taught to look for and "jump on" the next wave! It is this kind of thinking that has conditioned people to "enter into" the Mystical Revival. In Rodney's teaching on revival, the believer is likened to a surfer,

A surfer doesn't ride his board all the way to the white foam on the beach; he turns and paddles back, and looks for the next wave. But he doesn't take just any wave; he catches the right wave.[10]

Rodney Howard Browne's Views of What Is Coming

Predictably, Rodney Howard Browne sees the greatest revival ever seen about to break forth on the scene. In his book, **The Coming Revival**, Rodney sees a day coming when,

Eyeballs will form, legs and arms will grow out, people will leap out of wheelchairs. One of these days a true prophet, anointed of God, will be a guest on one of these television talk shows. When they start to mock him, he will simply look at them and say, "That you may know that there is a God who lives—that you may know that He shall not be mocked—you will be blind for three days as a sign to you and this audience." The talk show host will scream, "O my God, I can't see! I'm blind"...signs and wonders will be made manifest."[1]

Browne also asks us,

How are you going to take it when God begins to translate people? If God translated some of you from one city to another, you'd scream all the way to your destination. And when you arrived, they'd all get saved, just by taking one look at you.[12]

Holy Ghost Glue

In his book, **Manifesting the Holy Ghost**, he includes the following testimonial in his own unique, amusing way.

Holy Ghost Glue. When this happened I noticed a woman on the floor who was laughing uncontrollably. Then she started weeping and speaking in other tongues. She was lying on her back under the power of God with her hands—lying back above her head. She was stuck to the floor...The Mack Truck of God's power is coming! She was lying there from noon until 1:30 drunk in the spirit. At 1:30 she tried to get up. She wanted to get up. She couldn't. All she could do was flop her hands. So, she was there flopping away—flop, flop, flop, flop. She said, "I can't get up. I'm stuck to the floor."[13]

Try to picture the apostles doing this and laughing about it later! The absence of any apostolic testimony doesn't seem to trouble too many, unfortunately. The book goes on to tell us that,

The ushers told us later [after Rodney Howard Browne and the pastor went to lunch] that at 6 o'clock, the woman finally peeled herself off the carpet. Then it took her an hour to crawl from the center of the church auditorium to the side wall. She had been stuck to the floor for six hours![14]

This is Primarily About Spiritual Drunkenness

It is a mistake to think that the primary emphasis of this renewal is laughter. This is more about spiritual drunkenness, abandonment, and intoxication with the "new wine." Browne makes frequent references to Ephesians 5:18 and Acts chapter 2, when the mockers say, "These men are drunk on new wine." Browne in fact, refers to himself as God's bartender, and invites the people to have a drink at Joel's Place.

It is important to note, however, that Eph 5:18 refutes both drunkenness and the excesses that accompany it.

Eph 5:18-20 And be not drunk with wine, wherein is excess; but be filled with the Spirit; speaking to yourselves in psalms and hymns and spiritual songs, singing and making melody in your heart to the Lord; Giving thanks always for all things unto God and the Father in the name of our Lord Jesus Christ.

Being filled with the Spirit results not in ridiculous abandonment, but if anything, sober living, submission, alertness, clarity, thankfulness, the ability to teach and admonish one another. Eph 5:18 is a contrast with drunkenness rather than a higher parallel of it.

As for Acts chapter 2, we have to remember that it was the mockers who brought up the issue of drunkenness! If Peter would have had what these people have, he wouldn't have been able to preach his brilliant sermon explaining the recent events, from Psalms and Joel in which 3000 were converted.

Rodney tries to justify the confusion of his meetings by saying that wherever Jesus went, "pandemonium" broke out. As an example, he cites Mark 2:1-4, the story of the roof being torn off for the paralytic.

Mark 2:1-4 And again he entered into Capernaum after some days; and it was noised that he was in the house. And straightway many were gathered together, insomuch that there was no room to receive them, no, not so much as about the door: and he preached the word unto them. And they come unto him, bringing one sick of the palsy, which was borne of four. And when they could not come nigh unto him for the press, they uncovered the roof where he was: and when they had broken it up, they let down the bed wherein the sick of the palsy lay.

But you would be hard pressed to see in that story the drunkenness, ridiculous hilarity and confusion, that you see in a "Mystical Revival" meeting of today! Where is the howling, the people stuck to the ground, the others struck dumb? Jesus did rebuke some "laughers" at Jairus' home who broke out after he said, "the child is not dead but sleeps."

Quoting Tricia Tillin's excellent article in her Banner Ministry's **Mainstream**,

Surely Christian worship and ministry ought to be conducted in an orderly and reverent manner? Having said that, people will criticize us for being so tight laced and staid that we never let God do anything with us. Not so! Speaking for myself, I have attended many loud, boisterous, and joyful meetings, when people "let their hair down," but none of them was disorderly. There was no loss of control. The Holy Spirit, when he is allowed to take charge of our worship, will sometimes lead us to be exuberant (Ps 47:1) but he will never possess our bodies, causing unreasonable and uncontrollable physical reactions to occur.[15]

This is an excellent point. Did the Holy Spirit glue a woman to the floor for six hours, then force her to crawl for one hour across a single room? If so, why? We have to remember that the Holy Spirit didn't come to draw attention to himself, nor to man. Although it may have brought much amusement to the audiences and entertained the talk show hosts, how does "sticking a former Buddhist's rear end up in the air," draw glory and honour to Jesus? I don't get it, or I should say, I don't buy it.

Ministry Time

For an example of what "spirit" is being ministered at Rodney Howard Browne's meetings, look at the prayer I have transcribed from a service in Lakeland, Florida, as seen on "The Coming Revival" videotape. Alongside of the prayer I submit to you scriptures for consideration and discernment.

[RHB] "As you lift your hands say, "Lord fill me tonight, afresh with your fire, with your anointing, with fresh oil from heaven, *that the same fire that fell upon Brother Rodney in '79, let it fall upon me,* that the same fire that fell in the book of Acts fall upon me. I'm hungry Lord, I'm thirsty."

[Ed.] II Cor 4:5 For we preach not ourselves, but Christ Jesus the Lord; and ourselves your servants for Jesus' sake.

[RHB] "Now just close your eyes. *Don't pray.* Just close, *Don't pray...*Receive. I'm going to pray one simple prayer.

[Ed.] I Thess 5:17 Pray without ceasing.

[Ed.] Luke 18:1 And he spake a parable unto them to this end, that men ought always to pray, and not to faint.

[RHB] When I do, the power of God is going to hit this place. *It's tangible. Some of you will sense like electricity going through you, a fire, hot oil...like hot water going through you. Like a wind blowing right through me.* That's God's power. People sense the anointing in different ways. Get ready.

*[Ed.] Jude 19 These be they who separate themselves, **sensual**, having not the Spirit.*

[Ed.] II Peter 2:2 And many shall follow their pernicious [pernicious is sensual, literally] ways; by reason of whom the way of truth shall be evil spoken of.

[RHB] Lord, you told me, *"Son, give me an opportunity to move and I'll move."* And I give you an opportunity to move.

[Ed.] *Rom 11:34-35 For who hath known the mind of the Lord? or who hath been his counseller? Or who hath first given to him, and it shall be recompensed unto him again?*

[RHB] "Come!!! Now!!! There it is right now. There it is right now. The Power of God is beginning to fall. In the name of Jesus Christ of Nazareth be filled. Be filled...There it is all over this building. Right now the power of God is beginning to fall. *I loose the very touch of heaven* now, in Jesus' name...The fire of God is beginning to fall all over this place, all over this place...Just receive it...Like a river [8 times] Let it flow like a river."

[Ed.] *Isaiah 14:12-14 How art thou fallen from heaven, O Lucifer, son of the morning! how art thou cut down to the ground, which didst weaken the nations! For thou hast said in thine heart, I will ascend into heaven, I will exalt my throne above the stars of God: I sit also upon the mount of the congregation, in the sides of the north: I will ascend above the heights of the clouds; I will be like the most high.*

[RHB] "*Get your mind out of the way!* Let it bubble out of your belly, like rivers of living water. "These are not drunk as you suppose, but this is that which is spoken of by the prophet Joel." Let it bubble out of your belly like rivers of life giving water. Like a river. Yes. The new wine, [repeats the new wine 10 times]. It's joy unspeakable and full of glory! Thank you Jesus. That's right, let that bubble out of your belly [2 times]...Like rivers [5 times] *Don't worry about anybody else.* Like a river. [3 times]...Get 'em, Lord. Get 'em Jesus! Fill them up. What's happening to you? Need a dose, Lord..."

[Ed.] *Luke 10:27 And he answering said, Thou shall love the Lord thy God with all thy heart, and with all thy soul, and with all thy strength, and with all thy mind; and thy neighbour as thyself.*

[Ed.] *John 8:31-32 Then said Jesus to those Jews which believed on him. If ye continue in my word, then are ye my disciples indeed; And ye shall know the truth and the truth shall make you free.*

[Ed.] *I John 5:20 And we know that the Son of God is come, and hath given us an understanding, that we may know him that is true, and we are in him that is true, even in his Son Jesus Christ. This is the true God, and eternal life.*

[RHB] "This is a pastor of a church. This is a pastor of a church? *Lord, don't tickle him,* just bless him. *Drunk on the new wine. Drunk. Drunk. Drunk. Drunk. Drunk. Drunk. Drunk. Drunk. Drunk on the new wine.* Filled with the new wine. [2 times] Filled. Filled. Yes. Yes. Yes. Yes. Yes. Thank you Lord Jesus. Thank you Lord Jesus.

[Ed.] II Peter 2:17-18 These are wells without water, clouds that are carried with a tempest; to whom the mist of darkness is reserved forever. For when they speak great swelling words of vanity, they allure through the lust of the flesh, through much wantonness, those that were clean escaped from them who live in error.

[RHB] *That's one pastor between the pews. Hallelujah. have another drink, here sister. Have another drink.* What about you? Are you on vacation or something? Have a double dose.

[Ed.] Eph 5:4 Neither filthiness, nor foolish talking, nor jesting, which are not convenient: but rather giving of thanks.

[RHB] What do you think this is? You too. Filled. Have another round sister cocktailer, in the good sense of the word. Ha ha.

[Ed.] Matt 15:18 But those things which proceed out of the mouth come forth from the heart; and they defile the man.

[RHB] Have another drink over here. Go ahead. Filled. Filled. Filled. More. More. More. More. Drunk, I said drunk. I said drunk. I said drunk...

[Ed.] I John 4:5-6 They are of the world: therefore speak they of the world, and the world heareth them. We are of God: he that knoweth God heareth us; he that is not of God heareth not us. Hereby know we the spirit of truth, and the spirit of error.

[RHB] See people, you've got to yield. I said you've got to yield, you have to yield. You've got to not worry what others think about you. You've enough worry about your reputation. *People who get drunk and drink don't worry about what others think.*

[Ed.] Eph 5:3-7 But fornication, and all uncleanness, or covetousness, let it not be once named among you, as becometh saints; Neither filthiness, nor foolish talking, nor jesting, which are not convenient: but rather giving of thanks. For this ye know, that no whoremonger, nor unclean person, nor covetous man, who is an idolater, hath any inheritance in the kingdom of Christ and of God. Let no man deceive you with vain words: for because of these things cometh the wrath of God upon the children of disobedience. Be not ye therefore partakers with them.

[RHB] More. More. More. More. More. More. More. More. More...*They've got rid of their head also.*

[Ed.] Eph 5:11-12 And have no fellowship with the unfruitful works of darkness, but rather reprove them. For it is a shame even to speak of those things which are done of them in secret.

[RHB] All right. How many of you want prayer tonight, and hands laid on you? I'm going to be here until four in the morning. I can just see it. But I guess it's my fault because I opened Joel's Place. And people aren't going to leave until they've got a drink."

[Ed.] II Cor 6:17 Wherefore come out from among them, and be ye separate, saith the Lord, and touch not the unclean thing; and I will receive you.

To bring the precious Baptism of the Holy Spirit on the same level as a foolish, self-centered drinking binge is coming dangerously close to making a mockery of the Holy Spirit.

Heb 10:29 Of how much sorer punishment, suppose ye, shall he be thought worthy, who hath trodden under foot the Son of God, and hath counted the blood of the covenant, wherewith he was sanctified, an unholy thing, and hath done despite unto the Spirit of grace.

Challenging God!

Browne has an amazing little booklet out called **Walking in the Perfect Will of God**. The book starts out with a call to return to the fear of God, which I agree with. On page 1-2 Rodney states,

It amazes me that there is no fear of God in the church world today! People go out and do their own thing; it doesn't matter to them what Gods Word may say about it. They say, "I'm going to do my own thing. I'm going to do what I want to. God doesn't know." They shake their finger at Almighty God...

I agree, that it is appalling that puny man would ever dare to shake his finger at Almighty God! But the little booklet goes on to share Rodney's own personal commitment with God. His testimony starts out with him expressing frustration to the Lord. I'll let Rodney explain it, (starting at page 13).

To continue my story, we were driving along the highway and I was crying out to God desperately. Why? Because at that time in the ministry, the only preachers who were considered "successful" were the ones who had money and what money could buy.

No one ever emphasized how many souls were getting won. No one emphasized the characteristics of the anointing or the healing. They were just concerned about success. They thought you were the greatest preacher on planet earth if you had a nice suit and nice jewellery. I saw so many of those so called "successful" preachers running around looking like the image of success, but inside they were spiritually bankrupt. Nothing!

I said to the Lord, "It's not fair. You love those people more than you love me." (I am being honest about the way I felt.) Then I said, "God, there must be something they're not telling me." I said that because when I got into the inner circle, it was rotten to the core. Everything on the outside looked good, but the inside was rotten to the core.

And I said to God then and there, "God, if that is your will for the ministry, I, Rodney Howard Browne, don't want it. *You can have it*, because it's against what I feel in my heart is right.

What posturing! Isn't that nice? In effect saying, "God, I am above all that, even if you aren't." **"You can have it."** But that's not even the climax, read on and you will truly see the heart of this man exposed!

I was crying by then. My wife was crying. It was a powerful moment. I said, "God, I'm telling you right now, I'm giving you full permission to invade my life anytime of the day or night to straighten me out. But when I get to heaven and stand before you, if you look at me and say, "Rodney, you did not do my will," *I'm going to point my finger at You and say, "God, it's your fault,* because *I gave You* permission to come into my life and change me. *(From* **Walking in the Perfect Will of God***)*.

Now, remember, this isn't an example of an "off" night the evangelist was having, where he might have misspoken. This is a message he felt strongly enough to reproduce and put it in a book. Ironic that he progresses from lamenting the lack of fear of the Lord, to shaking his finger at God on Judgement Day!

In Conclusion

I suppose I could go on and on, "building a case," about my reservations of the ministry of Rodney Howard Browne, but why? After all of the above, if you don't have serious problems, you are also a victim of the continuous conditioning that has taken place. Keep in mind that it was a transference of his "anointing" into Randy Clark who brought "it" to Toronto, that "birthed" the Toronto Blessing. I hope that I have brought some clarity to the issue. This is not about personality, it's about truth. Can you see Jesus or the apostles even remotely promoting anything like this? I think not.

Is Rodney Howard Browne correct when he dismisses his critics by saying things like,

Now some would say, "I don't believe it," that's fine, those people that don't want to believe it, they probably wouldn't believe anything. They probably wouldn't believe the Bible...[16]

On the contrary, I don't buy this, and I believe in the Bible! I also believe in the present activity of the Holy Spirit. I consider myself to be spirit filled and have seen many "signs, wonders, and gifts of the Holy Ghost" over the years in my ministry as well as in many other fellow ministers. We have witnessed the casting out of devils, healing of the sick, and powerful life transformations, all to confirm the preaching of the gospel! So don't dismiss me as an unbelieving, religious dead head!

I want to close this chapter by encouraging you to hold fast to that which is good. We know that *certain men have crept in unawares*, but that doesn't mean that we have to throw out the validity of supernatural workings of God. The Pentecostal experience is needed now more than ever, God's people do need a fresh baptism in the Holy Ghost, to witness afresh to this sin-sick generation.

End Notes

1. July 21, 1994, Testimony Service Videotape. RHBEA Camp Meeting. Louisville, Kentucky.
2. Rodney Howard Browne. "The Touch of God." Page 71.
3. Ibid. Pages 73-74.
4. Ibid. Page 76.
5. Ibid. Page 100.
6. Julia Duin. "Praise the Lord and Pass the New Wine." Charisma Magazine. August, 1994.
7. Rodney Howard Browne. "The Coming Revival." Page 14.
8. Ibid. Pages 13-14.
9. Francis Frangipane. "Rising to Christ's Stature." Charisma Magazine. December, 1994.
10. Rodney Howard Browne. "The Coming Revival." Page 14.
11. Ibid. Page 27.
12. Rodney Howard Browne. "The Reality of the Person of the Holy Spirit." RHBEA Publications.
13. Rodney Howard Browne. "Manifesting the Holy Ghost." Pages 25-27. RHBEA Publications.
14. Ibid.
15. Tricia Tillin. "Is It Revival?" Mainstream. Summer, 1994. Banner Ministries Publication, Box 23, Belper, Derbyshire DE56 1QR, United Kingdom.
16. Bob and Molly DeAndrea. "The Good Life." Television Show. Florida. Date Unknown.

9
What I Saw in Toronto

I went to the Toronto Airport Vineyard for a first hand report. I attended several "renewal" services and interviewed many participants. It was especially interesting to interview pastors. It was a great experience for me. I would go to the services, listen to the beautiful worship music, the teaching and watch the ministry teams work. I could relate to so many involved. It was soon evident that many involved are quite sincere and truly believe they are involved in God's "new thing!" I could also relate to many on the basis that we had similar backgrounds in our Pentecostal Christian experience. Many who came to the "renewal" were fellow pastors, concerned about the dryness of the church, the apathy, prayerlessness, and lack of love. I could definitely relate to them. So having an empathy with many of the people, I can sincerely say that even though I am raising questions about the validity of the Toronto Experience, or Rodney Howard Browne, I don't believe for one minute that the people who are following this "wave" are bad people. In most cases, these people were sincere and dedicated Christians who simply are hungry and thirsty for God to move. So am I! I was touched late one night in the meetings when a team was called out of the service to go to downtown Toronto to feed the homeless. (Keep in mind also that this chapter is pretty subjective, it is my personal impression of what I saw and felt at Airport Vineyard in Toronto.)

A Typical Service

Walking into a worship service at the Airport Vineyard one Thursday night in December, 1994, I was struck first of all by the crowd. There were a couple thousand people there, of all ages, and social standings, lifting their hands in praise and worshipping, using many of the choruses that I am familiar with. It is a beautiful sight to see, a congregation in one accord, eyes closed, hands lifted, singing praises to God. This is what we all long for and it appeared to be what was happening here. One is struck by the young, actually rough looking kids, long hair, leather jackets, assorted ear and nose jewellery, yet lifting hands and singing of their love for Jesus.

Every once in a while, you would notice people twitching and jerking, some completely flailing their arms, a few laughing uproariously. Scattered throughout the congregation there were already many laying on their faces, oblivious to what was going on around them. I saw one lady who seemed to be trying to get up from a prostrate position, but was "stuck" in place! I've been around Pentecost all of my Christian life, so I was neither surprised nor dismayed by the "activity."

Testimony Time

After quite an extensive worship time and the offering, it was testimony time. The leader of the meeting repeatedly stressed that the manifestations are meaningless unless accompanied by a changed life. There were several called up to testify to the renewed spiritual life they had experienced since being touched in one of the services. One young man, who was a lawyer, told us that at first he felt out of place. He had expected the normal, dignified, suit and tie style church services. (In these services the mood is "laid back," frequently speakers have been known to be in jeans and t-shirts.) This young lawyer told us that he was sceptical until he too had been touched and went out under the power of the Spirit. He encouraged us to "soak," which means to repeatedly receive prayer and allow God to touch you. At the previous night's service, he testified that he had been healed of an asthmatic condition. After each testimony the one leading the service would pray for the one who testified, laying hands on that one and saying, "More Lord, more...more power Lord!" In almost every case I noticed, the one prayed for would manifest. This young lawyer went down and lay on the ground twitching, through the whole service.

Two Norwegian pastors were brought forward. Marc DuPont, the "prophetic minister" who was to speak, introduced the pastors to the congregation. The crowd was delighted when DuPont put his hand on one of the Norwegian's shoulders, causing him to be bowed over "under the power." This young Norwegian pastor was bowed halfway over, (forward, face down) and could not straighten himself up to testify. The crowd roared with laughter as this half bowed over Norwegian walked back and forth on the stage trying to stand erect, but unable to! He had to be helped to his seat, but on the way down to it, he fell over and jerked violently on the floor for much of the remaining service.

One thing I noticed, whenever there were manifestations in the front it would seem to touch a nerve with people through the crowd. As one person would "receive ministry" up front and manifest, people all over the crowd would jerk, twitch, laugh, moan, and convulse in response.

A "Prophetic" Message

After the testimony time, we were subjected to a message by Marc DuPont, an associate pastor at the Airport Vineyard, as well as a widely recognized travelling "prophetic" minister. DuPont opened up by telling us that the message he was about to deliver was so potent that God had told him to quit giving it for a while, unless specifically directed to, because too much happened. This message was primarily about knowing Jesus as the Lion of Judah and not merely as the Lamb.

It was a revealing sermon, considering that DuPont is recognized as one of the leaders of the Toronto Revival. As far as I'm concerned, the tone of the sermon was one of spite and contempt for the church as it is today. DuPont went so far as to tell us that God is bored with the church! He then quipped (joked) that the angels appointed to watch over us are so bored they went back to heaven and are now in counselling! (This is what I have seen and heard a lot in their doctrine, a sarcastic discontentment, a cynicism). Because these leaders are humorous, laid back, "humble," and seemingly concerned, this sarcasm can be quite effective, particularly with the young or irreverent. It looks like we have here a radical, iconoclastic, prophetic reformer!

DuPont also referred to Aslan, the lion character in C. S. Lewis' **Chronicles of Narnia**. Aslan the Lion, is Lewis' archetype of Jesus Christ. Using the story as a text, DuPont majored on one particular line from the story, where one character says to another, "Remember, Aslan is not a tame lion." DuPont sees in that a prophetic message to the church that Jesus is not tame, controlled, nor predictable. DuPont told how an unbelieving (in Aslan) dwarf in the story was surprised by the lion, thrown up in the air (loosing everything from his pockets) clothes and hair dishevelled and ultimately held still by Aslan, who looked him in the eyes and said, "Can we be friends now?" Supposedly, this is what God is doing in the pandemonium that people are calling the "Toronto Experience." DuPont has tagged 1994, "The Year of the Lion."[*1]

Another memorable aspect of DuPont's "prophetic teaching" was his alternately criticizing or defending sound doctrine. On the one hand, he would say, "Did God say, "My house shall be a house of Bible study?" " (as opposed to a "house of prayer") to which he would follow up, "I'm not saying we don't need doctrine and theology, we do!" DuPont would also stress the foolishness of seeking manifestations, but then offer countless examples of manifestations! In fact, he ended his sermon with a story of a visiting group of Japanese pastors, who at first were put off by the excesses of the Toronto meetings, but had been persuaded to stay for a while and soak. Toward the end of their stay, one of the leaders of the meeting felt compelled to ask a certain Japanese pastor to pray for him. Neither spoke the other's language, so finally the Japanese pastor stood back about five feet, grabbed out of thin air an imaginary ball of "power" and pitched it at the American pastor! This "ball" hit him in the stomach and knocked him over, intoxicating him with the "Spirit." The crowd loved the story for some reason and applauded it for a few minutes. As far as I'm concerned, that is as clear a demonstration as any of the occultic nature of many of these manifestations. Is God's blessing a force we can pull out of air at will and throw at someone? If so, why not just have a "save the world" snowball fight?

Before I close this section on DuPont's message, I will bring up one other aspect of it, for it was most disarming to the discernment of the people. DuPont put forth the idea that, "Most Christians have more confidence in Satan's ability to deceive us, than in the Holy Spirit to lead us and guide us into the truth." Whoever would question or discern, evidently is "bound by fear" or worse yet, is just a Pharisee. Doesn't that sound good? "Just let down your guard and trust God!" I do trust God, according to the Word. I trust the God who told us that in the latter times there would be a massive deception on a scale never known before! This theme comes out over and over in the leadership of the "Mystical Revival," "Quit being paranoid and jump into it! Turn off your mind, quit giving credit to the devil," etc. I hear the hiss of the serpent in it, "Let down your discernment."

Ministry Time: Come Holy Spirit

After the sermon, the chairs were stacked and removed for ministry time. You could feel the sense of expectation, something was about to happen. The ground rules were announced, "No one who doesn't have an approved ministry team badge can pray for people," also, "You are here to receive, so when you are getting prayed for, don't pray, in tongues or English for you are here to receive and that can hinder your reception." Hmmm. After the rules of engagement were announced, DuPont calmly invoked the Holy Spirit, "Come, Holy Spirit," and immediately people all over began to twitch, tremble, compulsively bend over face forward, and straighten up, over and over. Knees would give, arms would thrash, and some people would violently shake and quake. A few would become intensely cold and others feverishly hot! I saw a woman in her 50s laying on her back, suddenly convulse into a form of a sit up, rapidly and repetitively. Each time she would come up, out of her mouth would come the word "cuckoo!"

One older man, who looked Asian, was violently thrown to the floor by a spirit and flopped and thrashed, letting out a deep moan, (evidently a demon possession), oblivious to his surroundings. Just about every manifestation that I have described in this book, broke out in that one service as the people yielded to "the Spirit." Laughter, screams, moans and roars mingled together into an otherworldly cacophony. The ministry team, (a group of about 30 specially trained people) was released to begin praying for people. They would usually work in teams of two, one to stand behind the person to "catch" them, the other actually ministering in front of the person. These teams, by virtue of the number of them, could give as much time as needed to each seeker. They would pray for them, laying hands on forehead and belly, in some cases, fanning the "wind of the Spirit" or "splashing" the waves of the Spirit, onto the seeker. Usually, they would stay with the person till there was some kind of manifestation.

I had noticed a gentleman with shoulder length grey hair thrashing about the stage area on his back, even at times beating his head on the floor and side of the stage. He had commenced this even before the Spirit was invoked, and remained in that state for quite some time. I was amazed to find out during the following three services, he was the main speaker!

Calling All Bereans

We stayed till about 12:30 am. The ministry time was only beginning to wane at that point. On the way out of the auditorium, we struck up a conversation with two gentlemen, both of whom are ministers and both quite well known in certain circles. One of them was the author of a book on revivals that I had read.

[Me] "What do you think of all this?

[Him] "This is fresh, it's really needed."

[Me] "Don't you have any reservations?"

[Him] "Well, some of this is flesh and some of this is God, but at least something's happening."

[Me] "Don't you allow for the possibility of the "Delusion" spoken of in II Thess 2?"

[Him] "I never even think about that kind of stuff, it doesn't interest me and we aren't to be paralyzed by fear. All I'm concerned about is riding the next wave."

Then he really surprised me by continuing:

[Him] "Haven't you heard that when Rodney Howard Browne came to Oral Roberts University, Oral Roberts "Hit the deck?" [Was slain in the Spirit] I can see Richard going for something like this, but old Oral doesn't hit the deck for anyone."

[Me] "So that's how you confirm it?"

[Him] "Well, when Rodney Howard Browne came to Rhema, old man Hagin just sat there and wept and said, 'This is God!'"

I guess that settles it! Isn't that sad? There is a huge parting of the ways coming for the Pentecostals. For there are those who exercise no discernment other than their own subjective feelings. If a Charismatic media hero OK's it, it's all right. We weren't talking to a fresh faced young Christian convert, this was an author and an itinerant evangelist! By the way, I am not saying that Roberts or Hagin endorsed this phenomena, I am merely saying that this was the conversation we had, and this is the level of "discernment" that many have sunk to. "If Oral and Ken like it, it must be OK." Heaven help us! Are you beginning to see what Paul meant when he talked about people, *Who received not the love for the truth*, therefore were sent strong delusion that they should believe the lie and be damned?

That an alarming lack of discernment has become increasingly commonplace among Pentecostals became evident to me with great force up in Toronto. Many of the meetings I went to were still at the older facility the church had used, on Dixie Road. For these meetings you had to arrive two hours early, if you hoped to get a decent seat, and you had to stand in line and wait. This gave me a chance to talk to quite a number of people, notably, pastors from all over the USA. One young pastor was boasting about the fact that he hadn't preached a sermon in three weeks. The others around him praised God! Why hadn't he preached? He wasn't preaching because he was turning the service completely over "to the Spirit." There is coming an abandonment of all that smacks of order, tradition, and logic and reason.

Service Characterized by Drunkenness

At another service I attended, spiritual drunkenness seemed to be the predominant manifestation. After the invocation, "Come, Holy Spirit," the receptive congregation began to stagger and sway. Loud, raucous laughter rolled over portions of the congregation, like a wave. I was deeply concerned about one young family I met. It seems that they had been one of the founding families of a People of Destiny Church (Larry Tomczak) in Ohio, 14 years ago, but had grown disillusioned and left. Now, they had found "it" and were ready to take "it" back with them to Ohio. Such a lovely family, who obviously had come to the Lord and served Him. They were shocked that night after I had told them I didn't "buy it." I asked the dad, "Didn't you have any reservations at all, coming into this wave?" He emphatically replied, "No way, this is God! Two years of not feeling God is long enough!" At this time in the service the drunkenness has taken over the congregation! People are stumbling and falling over each other by the dozens. Most are flat on their backs with a silly dazed grin on their faces or trying to get up and unable to. One man was yelling at the top of his voice, another laying on the ground, feet straight up in the air, laughing and trying to get his feet down. The ministry team is going around "swishing" the wave on people, getting intoxicated themselves. I suppose in one sense this was "fun." It reminded me of my old days, high school "keg" parties, only wilder yet. The whole time this is going on, the young man from Ohio is telling me, "This is God," his eyes are bloodshot, he is swaying as he stands there, and he's breathing heavily, just about to fall over!

Another man I met there, was a young (middle aged) pastor who had left the Assemblies of God to "catch the wave." "Do you have any reservations?" I asked. His face broke into a "knowing" grin, "None whatsoever," he replied, "this is about shedding your inhibitions and removing your clothes, so to speak. At home I can take off my shirt and be who I really am and no one will criticize me. The Father is calling His kids home! Aren't you tired of being someone you are not? If we can't be who we really are with each other, then how are we ever going to reach the lost? So God seems to be breaking people down, making fools of them, and setting them free of their inhibitions, you know, removing their fig leaves." OH!

Who said inhibitions are bad? I don't want to plop down on my sofa wearing a t-shirt and my underwear! Inhibitions, in most cases, are God given! But he did pick up on one of the major themes there, the shedding of inhibition. David dancing in the ephod, or the people removing their garments to make a way for Jesus on Palm Sunday, are pointed to as examples of the openness that God wants to bring us into.

I am not implying that a physical immodesty is being promoted there, for I don't think that by any means. But the inhibitions that are being broken down are spiritual inhibitions. After all, how are you going to "go back" to orthodox Christianity, after you have prophesied in a lion's voice or "swum" in the River of Life on the floor in front of 3000 Christians? After the shedding of inhibitions like these, "coming back" becomes a more remote possibility than ever. Furthermore, you are more vulnerable (naked) to even more outrageous manifestations, after all, that little voice that says, "Don't go into this, it's improper," has been effectively silenced. In Toronto, I saw the evidences for a massive delusion that I believe is already here. People are being mystically initiated into a "new thing" and in many cases, they have been so conditioned to reject the past, tradition or head knowledge – critical thinking, they have been stripped bare of the last shreds of discernment that they had!

Saying the Right Things

This can be such a confusing phenomena to discern, for those involved say all of the right things at the right time. As I said earlier, the leadership will stress over and over again that this renewal is not about manifestations, or they will affirm that it isn't about "The Vineyard." But then they will turn around and call for testimony of the strangest manifestations, or they themselves will relate some strange story. I'm thinking for example, of a story Marc DuPont told on his tape, "Lion of Judah." There was an associate pastor at Wes Campbell's church, who collected doves. One young girl at the church asked him for a baby dove. He was so drunk in the spirit for 2-3 days, that it took him a half hour of attempts, trying to clip the baby dove's wings, (it usually takes about five minutes). After a half hour, he noticed his hands were covered with his own blood! Evidently, in his state of spiritual drunkenness, he had taken a full male dove and attempted to clip its wings and it had viciously bitten and ripped his hands. The crowd loved this story! DuPont says there is a prophetic word in this story, "We think the Holy Spirit is tame and gentle, but there's a whole new dimension we are about to see." Unbelievable!

Another thing that is stressed, which seems so good on the surface is the theme of love and romance with the Lord. They say, "The Lord is going to come to us as a lover." By that they aren't referring to His physical return rather, a spiritual coming. After being "touched" or manifesting the power, people are reporting that they have experienced a new "passion for Jesus." But what does it mean to love Jesus? Is having a passion for Jesus the same as loving Jesus? We love Him because He loved us first. Jesus said, "If you love me, keep my commandments." DuPont opened one of his messages this way, "I want to speak this morning on the heart of God…God a radical and jealous or zealous lover." He was speaking in ethereal terms of passion and romance, and abandonment.

The ultimate theme is the whole idea that "those of you who want your doctrine in order, God is going to turn over the tables." Typical and oft repeated lines like

DuPont's in his message "Lion of Judah," where he states, "Most Christians have more confidence in Satan and the Antichrist to deceive us, than they do in the Holy Spirit to lead us and guide us into the truth." John Arnott, in his comments on this trend, assures us that,

> The church is in reaction to fear right now, there have been books written about seduction and more seduction and people have read these books...I read those books for about three days and said, "What's the use?" People are always saying, "Be careful, be careful about going to Vineyard, I've heard they get really emotional." There is a fear of emotion, a fear of deception. Now, let's see, hands up, all those who want to be deceived...[crowd laughter]...No, we don't want to be deceived, but neither do you want to live your life in reaction, living under a fear of deception...It's time that the church had more faith in God's ability to bless us than Satan's ability to deceive us... *(from his tape, "Receiving the Spirit's Power).*

It is not fear to have a healthy respect for the warnings Jesus gave us.

Matt 24:4, 10-11 And Jesus answered and said unto them, Take heed that no man deceive you. And then shall many be offended, and shall betray one another, and shall hate one another. And many false prophets shall rise, and shall deceive many.

The Bible also teaches us that the heart itself can deceive you. People who believe all the warnings and promises in the Word of God are not "bound by a spirit of fear." *Jer 17:9 The heart is deceitful above all things, and desperately wicked: who can know it?* Of course we are so aware of the possibility of deception!! When leaders like Arnott would ridicule this concept, get the crowd laughing about it, and chide the church for having a healthy respect for Jesus' warnings, not to mention the warnings of the apostles. One of the surest guarantees of deception is the assurance that you can't possibly ever be deceived.

There was an overall irreverence exhibited at the meetings. People felt the liberty at times to interrupt testimonies, with humorous (?) comments. At a very solemn appeal for salvation, one Sunday morning, uncontrollable and uproarious laughter seemed to grip some in the congregation. A pastor went forward for prayer and his parishioner (evidently) stood up and waved at him and said, "Bye bye, Pastor," implying that he would soon be going down under the power. Overall, there was a lighthearted, carnival atmosphere. Even ministry teams would pray for one person who erupted in laughter, then would "come after" those who amusedly looked on.

The overall feeling was "party time." Indeed, many involved would tell you, "We are partying with the Lord." Of course, young people are attracted to it!

This chapter is my experience and impression of what is called the Toronto Renewal. The next chapter is written to take a closer look at some of the prominent leaders and influences, and what they are saying.

*1 See Appendix B.

10
Toronto Leaders Speak for Themselves

The best and fairest way to try to put the Toronto Blessing in context would be to allow the leadership to speak for themselves. I have selected a sampling of quotes on a variety of subjects from a small handful of leaders. I will not necessarily offer counter comments on all of these. Suffice to say that some of the things said here I agree with and some I disagree with. The leaders I have selected to quote are by no means the only leaders of this movement, for there are many. In many ways, this truly is a "nameless, faceless movement," as John Arnott told **Charisma Magazine**. There will be some comments to which I will reply, but briefly, as the rest of the book pretty much covers that ground. I urge you, as you read this, to consider two things. Number one, it is your responsibility to be a Berean and search the scriptures for yourself to see if these things be so. Number two, when it comes to examining a ministry or movement, the external manifestations are secondary, the main thing to examine is the message and its content!

John Arnott

As pastor of Airport Vineyard, John Arnott and his church have been host to six day a week services continuously since January, 1994. As of December 1, they have had at least 100,000 visitors from Canada, the United States, and all over the world! Six thousand of those visitors have been pastors, seeking to get a touch of God and to take that touch home with them!

Arnott on God's Purpose in this Revival

I have consistently heard John Arnott stress that the purpose of this visitation is in accordance with Revelation, in reference to restoring our first love. This visitation is more of a renewal for the church than a revival (at this stage), which would result in the mass conversion of the lost. That is not to say that people aren't being saved, according to them. But the people in Toronto, including Arnott prefer to call this a refreshing or a renewal because it is primarily dealing with Christians. Ultimately, they hope it will result in conversion of the lost.

[Arnott] When it first broke out on us, I was so anxious to, "Let's get on with evangelism." I didn't understand the purposes of God in what He had particularly for us here,...God has got a different dynamic going...God is renewing the church and then empowering the church to probably go and gather the greatest harvest the world has ever seen. *(From his tape, "Receiving the Spirit's Power.")*

Arnott on Hinkle's failed June 9th Prophecy

It's always revealing, the attitudes people have about critical thinking. A common problem with leadership today is their refusal to criticize or judge the false. This is certainly a tragedy. We need strong leadership more now than ever! A prime example is John Hinkle's prophecy. He prophesied that on Thursday, June 9th, the Lord would rip all evil off the face of the earth. That "prophecy" was later spiritualized and revised to say that the "spiritual veil of darkness would be torn, allowing people to see the light!" The Kansas City Prophets and others allegedly had received "words from God" to the effect that for New Testament times, the standard for prophets was different than Deut 18. According to them, a "prophet" can be 40% inaccurate and still be considered valid! Unfortunately, thanks to people like John Wimber, their teachings have been widely accepted. You can see this lax view of prophetic standards in this Arnott observation! The following quote may well have been made before June 9th.

[Arnott] People get funny when things like this happen...June 9th, there was a prophecy given by a reputable man,...that the Lord would tear open the veil, the shroud of darkness that is over the earth, that is blinding the earth, and as He tore the veil of the temple when Jesus arose, now He's going to tear open the heavens and allow the glory of God to come down...I really hope it comes true...I know that He's up to something...Don't get too excited about dates, sometimes prophetic people are right about the event, but **wrong about the date.** [emphasis mine]

(I'm glad Daniel, Jeremiah, or Isaiah were never wrong about details in their prophecy. Speaking inaccurate things in the name of being a prophet may indeed no longer require the death penalty, but the sin is no less serious!)

Arnott: God's Getting Us Used to Him

We have had word after word about "get ready, cause you're just on the hors d'oeuvres right now," but the power is coming. We've had a word that said, you know, "I'm just going easy on you now with this kind of stuff so you can kind of get used to me and acclimatize, because when the real power shows up I don't want you to be terrified!" (From receiving the Spirit's power).

How Arnott Learned to Receive

Arnott is very candid in his tape, "Receiving the Spirit's Power," about how he had a hard time receiving, due to control, analysis, and fear. He relates in the tape how he had his friend, Benny Hinn, pray for him 50 times, and yet he never "went down under the power." Even if he did "go down" at a public meeting, the whole time he would be analyzing the experience, "Is that you God? Or me? Was I pushed, did my knees cave in, or what?" kind of thing. On the other hand, he believed his wife Carol was the most sensitive person in the Holy Spirit he had ever met.

Eventually, he got to the point where he asked her how this business of receiving from the Spirit really worked:

"I finally start to ask Carol, "Honey, what do you feel?" (Carol), "Oh, it's just wonderful." (Arnott), 'Well, help me," you know, and so she says, "Now, just tune in," and so I'd be tuned in and I'm there, going like this,...and maybe I'd even start weaving a little bit, and I'm thinking "Lord, do I feel something on my hands or am I just making this up? Is there something here or am I so wanting this?"...And Carol would say, "No, no, I can feel Him going in, I can feel Him going in, Just keep focused!" You know and then...she'd say, "Oops, where did you go?" I'd say, "What do you mean?" She'd say, "I feel it coming back on me, where did you go?" And I would realize my mind had drifted off again someplace. *("Receiving the Spirit's Power")*

(Did the apostles teach union with God through mental focus? Can you imagine Peter or Paul discerning the Lord "going in someone," then rebuking them for not focusing after feeling the Lord "coming back out?")

On the Fear of Who Prays for You

Arnott has strong feelings about the church, "reacting in fear," as I quoted in an earlier chapter. To him, the church has an unreasonable fear of deception, fear of intimacy, fear of emotion, and in this case, fear of the wrong people laying hands on you.

[Arnott] Don't react by even who's praying, I get so tired of people saying, "Be careful who's praying for you now, somebody might lay hands on you that's not really free, and you might get something you didn't bargain for" [crowd laughs]. Listen, you know what Jesus did? He'd walk right up to a leper and lay hands on him, He wasn't afraid of getting leprosy!"

and

Don't worry about who's praying for you, my goodness, there's not a perfect person praying for people on the face of the earth!

On Intimacy and Emotion

Arnott has a particular theme that he, DuPont and many of the others continually refer to, which is romantic intimacy with Jesus. I don't think that passionate love for Jesus is a faulty theme, I myself am passionate in my love for Jesus. However, how much did Jesus himself actually call people to concentrate on passionate romance for Him? How do you measure love for Christ? What does "a radical love affair with Jesus" mean?

[Arnott] Men, if you're out looking for a bride, how would you like one who said, "Well, I'll sign a contract with you and I'll agree to all of those doctrinal items, but I will not be emotional with you ever. I won't hug you, kiss you, love you, any of that because I don't believe in emotionalism."

What an absolutely ridiculous analogy based on sensuality! I've never met any Christians like that. Why is it that doctrinal allegiance always has to be tarred with the brush of being sterility, stuffiness, and lovelessness? This next quote tells us that when it comes to the passionate love they speak of, don't analyze, just go for it!

The Holy Spirit wants to come and have intimacy with you—This is not the time to analyze...We've told hundreds of people, "Look, it's all about romance, it's not about analysis at all,' and so when someone whom you really love, your husband, your wife, your friend, whatever, comes near to you and they're kissing you, that's not the time to analyze..."Ooh, why are they putting their mouth to my mouth? Don't they know there's more germs in the human mouth than any other part of the human body?" [crowd laughter]...You'd ruin the moment, right? ("Receiving the Spirit's Power").

The Bible speaks much of those who are sensual, who lead people astray, they manipulate people by appealing to their discontent, dry times, or lack of "feeling God." Sensuality doesn't always refer to the use of the five senses, in knowing God. The mystics were sensual, striving to base their unity with God on feeling Him, or seeing, hearing, and even smelling Him. This present move is a mystical and sensual revival.

Arnott on What to Expect

People ask us all the time, "What do you feel?" and that's a valid question. At first, it's almost imperceptible, but you think your hands are feeling a little heavier, this is my experience, and as you love Him, and stay tuned to that and say, "Oh, Lord, more of your presence," and it gets heavier and they begin to tingle, kind of, sort of like electricity and it can flow all up and down your arms and all over your face and up and down your legs and when it really increases, it's like you're being electrocuted, almost.

Jude 19-20 These be they who separate themselves, sensual, having not the Spirit. But ye, beloved, building up yourselves on your most holy faith, praying in the Holy Ghost. James 3:15 This wisdom descendeth not from above, but is earthly, sensual, devilish.

Arnott—On the Animal Noises

Animal noises coming from people is an increasingly common phenomena in the Toronto Blessing. The leaders are having to give some pretty interesting interpretations to them.

The following quote is taken from a question and answer session from the Wednesday, October 19, 1994, Pastor's Meeting audio tape. The question is unclear, but as you will see from John Arnott's answer, he is explaining the animal noises phenomena.

[Arnott] All of the animal sounds are really interesting. A challenging question. Our official answer is, we don't know why people do that. [crowd laughter]...If you eliminate the possibilities, it's either demonic, or it's the flesh, or it's the Holy Spirit. Those are the three options I think, right? So assuming it's the Holy Spirit, then what could He possibly be doing? And therefore, we see it as a prophetic message of some point. And always, the person will tell us how strong they felt. Did you feel His great strength going into you at the same time?

Answer unintelligible. [Couldn't hear it].

[Arnott, in reply.] So, you felt great strength and greatly empowered, so it's kind of a Samson anointing for strength. I don't know what sort of noises Samson made when...he carried the gates to the top of the hill...he didn't just go, "Oh, well, let's just do this quietly."...He probably made this great roar...as he was empowered...it's a natural impulse when people are going to war...because it's the stronger spirit that wins as they say in karate.

Arnott goes on to explain that the roaring as lions and other animal noises tie in prophetically with Hosea 11:10 and Amos 3:6-7 and incredibly—with the cherubim of Revelation 4!

[Arnott] It's highly speculative and uh, very immature and undeveloped at this stage, but I'll pass on some thoughts I had, if you want to turn to Rev 4. We're in the throne room of heaven. Now, one of the criticisms, even from within the Vineyard, OK, is that for human beings made in the image of God to make animal sounds is degrading and a slam against their integrity...The Holy Spirit would never do that. What we're seeing is the animals themselves as a prophetic statement about the glory of God.

Arnott launches into a description of the four cherubim in Revelation 4, the one with the face of an eagle, lion, ox, and man.

[Arnott] And so now we're starting to see people prophetically acting like lions, and oxen, and eagles, and even warriors. We had a phone call one time it said, "One of our congregation's been acting like an eagle, flying around the room. We can't get them to stop, what do we do?" And we thought, you know, throw a rabbit out in the middle of the floor and maybe they'll come down." [crowd•laughter] "But seriously, it's a wonderful thing...we've seen it spontaneously in Steve Wood's church, from St. John New Brunswick on the east coast, we had all four of those manifestations happening at the same time...What did the man look like? He looked like a warrior, just yelling, "Ahhhh!!!," you know. You see that, our first inclination is "that's demonic!" But that is too simplistic a view...It scared people so bad that many of them ran right out of the meeting...This little keyboard player lady, about 115 lbs, she's on all fours, just snorting and pawing the ground like an angry bull. That went on for a while and she's frightened...she ran out of the room at one point. Carol went after her and we encouraged her, "You're ok. Just let the Lord do what He wants to do. You asked for bread, after all, He's not going to give you a stone." *(Transcript from Wednesday, October 19, 1994 Pastor's Meeting. Airport Vineyard. Toronto, Ontario).*

Arnott goes on to say that at a leadership meeting with John and Carol Wimber, to discuss the problem, John Wimber concludes that there just isn't enough spiritual ground to support that kind of phenomena. It was at this point, according to Arnott, that Carol Wimber interjected.

[Arnott] And his wife Carol, as only she could do in her way, is saying, "Well, wait a minute, John. If Jesus wants to bring His friends to the party, don't you think we should let Him?" That's good isn't it?..."So if He wants to bring the cherubim from before the throne, and they're...manifesting through different people of integrity, roaring and flying and all that, I don't know." *(October 19, 1994. John Arnott, Pastor's Meeting. Airport Vineyard, Toronto. Audio Transcript).*

I could go on, but I think you get the point. John Arnott is the pastor of the Airport Vineyard, and one of the primary leaders of this revival. These are his own words. There are a few others who have been influential in the propagation of the Toronto experience.

Marc DuPont

Marc is an associate pastor at the Toronto Vineyard as well as a widely travelled conference speaker, and much in demand. He is considered a "prophetic minister," in fact, a year before this outbreak, he prophesied extensively that it was coming! That prophecy is recorded in Guy Chevreau's book **Catch the Fire**.

On This Current Move

It's always interesting to hear the perspectives on what is currently happening at Toronto and worldwide. DuPont has labelled 1994, "The Year of the Lion," after God had given him Amos 3:6-7. DuPont is also quite outspoken about his belief that God is partying with His people.

DuPont, "God is throwing a party right now and giving free food, which is Himself..." DuPont has another unique interpretation of what God is doing. DuPont, "This move of the Spirit is not just a Charismatic and Pentecostal experience concerning power or gifting. It is one thing to be clothed with power it is another to be indwelt with the person of God."

DuPont on the Church

Listening to Marc DuPont for very long, will leave you with either a cynical or at least a discouraging impression of the church. When I heard him preach December 1, 1994, he told us that God was bored with the church. In one of his tapes, he told us that when we bring people to church with us, "instead of seeing people drinking on the new wine, they see a bunch of people who have been mainlining on prunes." And, of course, the old "you haven't been fed" charge is given a new twist, "We've been eating, old, maggot infested, dried out bread and we say this is revelation." Incredibly, this kind of cynicism can be quite effective in its impact on people, opening them up to discontentment. DuPont seems to be quite concerned about Christians becoming too doctrinal. He's also one of the voices chanting the tired mantra, "Christians have more faith in Satan and the Antichrist's ability to deceive us than the Holy Spirit's to lead and guide us into all truth." His answer to that danger, "We have to trust more in our hearts than in our heads—and that is very scriptural—Prov 3:5-6. Jesus never said your theology would lead you and guide you into all truth. The Spirit will lead you." It is not scriptural at all to tell people to trust in their hearts, (Jer 17:9). The scripture says, *Trust in the Lord with all your heart and lean not to your own understanding.* In another amazing statement Marc DuPont accuses the church, that "We love the truth about Jesus more than we love Jesus Himself." (from the tape "Lion of Judah.")

DuPont can say so much in one statement, just by implication. Let's examine one statement, from his tape "Holy Ghost Train." "God is raising up a slightly different army of evangelists, motivated by the Father's compassion rather than those motivated by cold, hard numbers, of either going to Hell or going to Heaven." Are you implying that up till now, evangelists have been "motivated by cold, hard numbers?" Supposedly, **we** are different, **we** have compassion! Come on! I've never met any evangelist who was motivated by anything other than sheer love, this isn't some "slightly different" army, or some new thing! Rather, these be they that separate themselves!

The Mark of Marc

Marc DuPont believes that it's the Spirit of God that is doing the violent, frightening manifestations that so many are experiencing. Once again, from the tape, "Holy Ghost Train."

> God is not a gentlemen, God is God! God is not the great I was or I will be, right now, the dirty now and now. Not the sweet by and by...Quite often, when God's spirit comes it's a little more than crazy, how the Son of God comes on people! I've seen glasses fly across the room, I've seen marriage rings flying off fingers, I've seen boots and shoes flying off people, we've seen people destroy their clothes, almost being thrashed by the Holy Spirit!

In a service that was actually led by Wes Campbell, Marc DuPont felt led to "move in the prophetic," calling selected men forward to be "ambassadors for the Kingdom of God" to other pastors and leaders in the Body of Christ because "it's not a Vineyard message it's a kingdom message, what God is doing."

> Many leaders are going to be greatly shaken, I think that means not just theologically, but as already happening, many are being shaken in the spirit, it's happening quickly, talk about paradigm shifts, many people are just losing their paradigms and that's what needs to happen...I believe God wants to put a mark on many of you, even right now...He wants to put a mark upon you, I believe the Lord is going to start challenging you to contact other pastors and leaders that you've had relationship with in the past where maybe there's been rocky turmoil things...God's going to want to use some of you to be ambassadors for what He's doing here, because He's wanting this to go to other churches...I believe the Lord is going to put a mark on some of you and He's going to put a burden within you for some other pastors, Lutheran, Baptist, whatever...We're going to, uh, I see in the Spirit the angel, an angel, I don't know if it's the angel of the Lord, but angels are going to come and the Holy Spirit is going to put a cross on some of you...

On a tape featuring Wes Campbell, Marc is called forward to pray for a few of the pastors. During the ministry time, Marc proclaims that he is "placing a mark" on them, prophetically! This is certainly a mystical practice, what "mark" could he be talking about?

Wes Campbell

Another person who has been an influential voice, relating to this mystical revival, is Wes Campbell. Wes is the pastor of New Life Vineyard Fellowship of Kalowna. He came from a Plymouth Brethren background who says he often would use John MacArthur's anti-Charismatic sermons, as a Baptist pastor. During a time of seeking for renewal, he found himself attending Vineyard Conferences. His worship leader attended a conference in Anaheim where, according to Campbell, "He was hit by the Spirit, and began to shake and bounce...for three to four hours at a shot." After going to see another pastor, to get prayer for this man, he began to bounce so violently, his glasses and his wedding ring flew off. Campbell said in a sermon, "His wife was afraid, my wife was afraid. I liked it." In the course of time, he says that the Lord began to release "strong manifestations of shaking and prophecy" into his conservative congregation. All of this broke out in 1988, but amazingly, Campbell himself had almost no manifestations himself. He believes that God used his sobriety, to allow him to be a "traffic director," and eventually to become an apologist for the movement.

It was Wes Campbell who produced the aforementioned paper, **Prophet Sharing, 1992, Spiritual and Physical Manifestations**. This paper was written to answer the questions that would inevitably arise, such as, "Why all this shaking and what is its purpose?" Under the first heading, **Are Spiritual and Physical Manifestations Biblical?** Campbell replies,

> In a sense that is a loaded question in that it may be asking if an issue can be proven by scriptural proof, or if the issue is acceptable based on scriptural principle. Of course, proof is always easier, but often in our Christian walk things are not that clear cut. More often than not the Bible tells us "what" to do but not "how." It states "absolutes," but not "forms." Hence in the 16th century, many reformers destroyed the church organs because they were not, quote, "found in the Bible." Of course, we know that this type of hermeneutic (means of interpreting the scripture) is faulty. So, to answer the question, are manifestation in general (ie shaking with prophecy) biblical? Yes. Is there a specific text for it? No.

Do you see what he did there? I hardly think there is a comparison between what is happening in Toronto being questioned, and reformers destroying organs because they don't see them in scripture! The one is obviously ridiculous, because the scripture plainly tells us to worship God. But to imply that it is just as ridiculous to challenge these manifestations, on the basis of scripture, is unfair. Campbell does give a smattering of texts to look up however, I Samuel 10:19, 19:20, and Acts 2:2, 4:31.

In the same paper, Campbell attempts to anticipate possible objections that people may have to these manifestations. His answers to these objections are quite revealing. For example, Objection #2 states that, **shaking produces fear and misunderstanding. That does not feel like God**. To this he replies,

> Of course manifestations scare people precisely because they are of God. Every time God or the glorified Son appears, the reaction is immediate fear followed by an explanation and word of comfort *not to fear*. **Why? Because the observer was in total fear...Moses and the people at the mountain; Daniel 10; John; Rev 1:17, Gideon; Judges 6:23; Exodus 20:18-21...Whoever said that God's presence should only bring peace doesn't know God's presence.**

The last few lines of this particular section speak volumes about where these people are coming from. Immediately after the last line, concerning knowing God's presence, Campbell declares, "Let those who have communed with Him speak. **Paul Cain** and others." Those who have communed with Him? Paul Cain? These are the ones who are qualified to speak out about God's presence, in this view, for these are the ones who have actually "communed with God." Whatever happened to, *In that day...all shall know the Lord, from the least to the greatest?*

In a tape recorded at the Airport Vineyard, Wes Campbell reminisced about the early times when "the Spirit" first began to manifest through shaking and prophecy in his church. Evidently, those were times when you could get questions you had answered by God through people who were under this anointing.

One of the things that the Lord said to us through prophetic unction when this first happened was "Why does God shake people?"...'Cause we asked Him, there were times when the Lord would move on different ones, and we could literally, in the early days, ask questions, they would prophesy and we would just say, "God why does this happen?" And then the answer would come through prophetic unction, and we would ask this. Why do we do this? And this would come through answer.

I believe in the gift of prophecy, but to inquire of God through a human being in the manner described above, makes that person into a channel, or an oracle. God doesn't work that way. The anointing of the Spirit doesn't come on people so that God can answer questions through their voice. Judge the answer, that this "Spirit" gave them.

The second night He said this, He said, "I have come to you through...my Word and I tell you everything for life," and He says, "And you don't listen"...Then He said this, "I've come through prophetic word and I've spoken, and you don't listen,"...And all of the sudden, He went on David and He says (with emphasis) "And now...I shake you!...And now you will listen!"

Supposedly, God revealed to these people, that since we won't listen to His written Word, or to the gift of prophecy, He has to physically shake us to get our attention! How did they learn this? Through a prophesied answer to a question, that was asked of God.

There is so much more we could say, I'm just trying to give you a feel for where these people are coming from. Judge for yourself! Listen to them, hear what they are saying. I can't for the life of me figure out how people can openly state such positions and go relatively unchallenged. Can you see the mysticism being promoted? The faulty hermeneutics? The abandonment of the faith once and for all delivered? Heaven help us!

Let me close this chapter with a discussion of excerpts from Guy Chevreau.

Catch the Fire

Guy Chevreau came out of the Baptist church. After a few years of preaching ministry, a hunger for more of "kingdom power" began to develop in his life. Before long, he was impacted by a church growth seminar featuring Mike Turrigiano, who told of his inner city ministry, which included outreach to heroin addicts, prostitutes, much prayer for the sick, healing and deliverance. It was at this point that he read Wimber's **Power Evangelism** and **Power Healing** and began to shed his "de-supernaturalized" perspective.

Along with Wimber's books, I was reading other church growth material: on leadership, innovation, infrastructure, time management, goal setting, and strategic planning, *paradigm shifts* and mission philosophy...Several years later, I resigned from a traditional, parish-based ministry and moved to a church plant setting, where it was hoped that we would have greater freedom to grow as a church that was unapologetic in its purpose: to be a supernaturally gifted and missioned community of faith, gathered to reach the unchurched through intentional relationship evangelism." (*Catch the Fire*, Page 12).

The new church he started was soon determined to not be viable and by June, 1994, it was closed down.

But in January, 1994, his wife, Janis, told him about the "outbreak" of spiritual drunkenness at Airport Vineyard. Then he tells how he came to **Catch the Fire**.

The next night, we came to the Airport meeting. I came more desperate than curious, and too desperate to be critical. As a Baptist pastor, I personally had not seen anything much by way of physical manifestation of the Spirit's power or presence...It is an understatement to say that I was personally unfamiliar with the kinds of physical manifestations we saw at the Airport meetings—uncontrollable laughter and inconsolable weeping; violent shaking and falling down; people waving their arms around, in windmill like motions, or vigorous judo like chopping with their forearms. (*Catch the Fire, Guy Chevreau, Page 13. Marshall Pickering*).

It was Chevreau's wife who first "took the joy." In fact, he tells us that Pastor Arnott prayed for her repeatedly, leaving her "on the floor, hysterical with laughter." Pastor Arnott actually prayed for her that she would stay that way, "in that state" for 48 hours. According to Chevreau,

She was that, and more—at times unable to walk a straight line, certainly unfit to drive, or to host the guests that came for dinner the next evening. Typically, she is able to prepare the meal ahead of time so that we can focus our energies on those visiting. When I returned home from work that particular night, the kitchen looked very unready for dinner—there was no food in sight, and when I asked about the meal, Janis nearly fell to the floor in hysterical laughter. I went out to buy fish and chips. On my return, our guests were already seated at the table. Without any place settings, Janis proceeded to toss hot, greasy fish to each of us; she dumped the box of french fries in the middle of the table, and then pushed little piles in our respective directions, all the while finding everything very funny. (*Catch the Fire*, Page 14).

This is a testimony, not of one who is questioning this move, but of an ardent supporter. **Catch the Fire** is the definitive book concerning Toronto. I thought the Spirit was poured out to empower us to serve others! This drunkenness is more and more revealed as an exit into self absorption.

As an example of this kind of testimony, Chevreau felt he should include in this book, a testimony of the healing of a pastor's daughter, of dyslexia:

[She] has struggled with dyslexia for her entire school career. [She is 13 years old].

From her early youth she had problems processing what she heard, and understanding both written and spoken words. Reading has always been very difficult. She often felt "left out" because of her inability to understand much of a conversation; she found it very hard to understand directions.

In Toronto, she asked for prayer for her learning disability. We had been there four nights and had been getting ministry at every opportunity. Heather had many times, during and after prayer, shaken and jerked, and sometimes done dramatic dance-like movements. When she received prayer for dyslexia, she fell to the floor, very still. Later she told us that angels had done brain surgery. She heard God instructing them, and was told to be very still, because "This is delicate surgery." She also reported that one of the angels got so excited that she began playing with Heather's brain, and that God had to calm her down, saying, "This is very serious, and not the time for play." (She thought that was funny). She felt herself on a cold operating table, and at the end, saw a picture of herself praying for other friends with dyslexia." (*Catch the Fire*, Page 171).

This girl's younger sister who is also labelled dyslexic, reported,
"The angels shaved my head, across the top of it from ear to ear. Then they cut my head, pulled the front of it open, and took out my brain." She drew a picture of how her brain looked, with a concave, indented area. 'That is what the angels worked on, pulling that out to be curved, like the rest of my brain. Then they put it back in my head and I could feel the tug of stitches, across the top of my head." (*Catch the Fire*. Page 172).

I can only see one of two possibilities here, for where these "testimonies" have come from. Either these girls have a tremendously active (and morbid) imagination, or something demonic has happened to them. God has to cut your head open to heal you? He has to tell you to hold still, for Him to operate? He then has to rebuke an angel who plays with your brain? The main point, is not so much the stories the girls told, but that Chevreau, one of the chief chroniclers of this revival, actually picked them out of the thousands available, he used them for an authentication of this move. This is an example of the level of insight and discernment we have come to.

11
On Spiritual Drunkenness

Why This Revival is not a Laughing Matter

You may have observed by now, that though it is often tabbed "The Laughing Revival," this movement isn't really so much about laughter as it is about spiritual drunkenness. After all, Rodney Howard Browne doesn't call himself the "The Laughing Evangelist," but he does refer to himself as "God's Bartender," and bids the people to come drink at "Joel's Place!" The prophets and leaders up in Toronto, likewise speak of "partying in the Lord." "God's throwing a party now and food and wine are free."

How are we to interpret spiritual drunkenness? What are we to make of "partying with God?" Is this a biblical concept? No doubt, it feels good, but is it really God honouring? To put the question in a different light, did Jesus and the disciples ever "turn people on" to this kind of intoxication? Can we really equate spiritual drunkenness with fullness of the Holy Spirit? I hope to fully explore these and other related aspects, and also to offer a biblical perspective of this experience for you to judge by.

Spiritual Drunkenness is Biblical

It is true, that the Bible speaks of the condition touted as "drunk in the Spirit." But the interpretation, the significance of it, is different than the current one. The Old Testament prophets as well as Jesus and the apostles did speak of the phenomena, but warned of it as a judgement from God on an unbelieving people, which it would blind, deafen and render useless those so afflicted. The biblical descriptions of spiritual drunkenness given by the prophets are striking in their similarity to the manifestations I have seen in services and on videos.

Moses, for example, warned about the "man, woman, family or tribe" whose heart would turn away from the Lord to go after other gods, because of bitterness and discontent. Moses warned us that that one would actually "bless himself in his heart saying, "I shall have peace though I walk in the imagination of my heart," and would go on to, "add drunkenness to thirst." (See Deut 29:18-21). We have a lot of people today, who have drifted away from the God of the Bible, to worship and seek the presence of a god who exists in their own imaginations. But they have learned to "bless themselves" in their hearts, or reaffirm to themselves that everything's all right. Because they have left off the fountain of living waters, to drink out of broken cisterns that can hold no water, a tremendous spiritual thirst has developed. But have they turned in repentance back to the God of the Bible? No way, that's "bondage," "doctrinal," and even "religious." Instead of doing that which would humble them, they have responded to thirst with drunkenness, exactly as Moses foretold.

Isaiah also speaks of this phenomena in stark terms.

Isaiah 28:7-8 But they also have erred through wine, and through strong drink are out of the way; the priest and the prophet have erred through strong drink, they are swallowed up of wine, they are out of the way through strong drink; they err in vision, they stumble in judgement. For all tables are full of vomit and filthiness, so that there is no place clean.

Notice, it is the strong drink and the wine that caused the people to err, and go out of the way. Even the priest and the prophet "err in vision and stumble in judgement." I think that this is an extremely important thing to note, for much of the leadership of this "Mystical Revival" are composed of those who consider themselves to be prophets. Even if it were true that they are prophets, Isaiah warns us that those who participate in this become blind and go into error!

Isaiah is even stronger in his denunciation of this in his next chapter.

Isaiah 29:9-14 Stay yourselves, and wonder; cry ye out, and cry: they are drunken, but not with wine, they stagger, but not with strong drink. For the Lord hath poured out upon you the spirit of deep sleep, and hath closed your eyes: the prophets and your rulers, the seers hath he covered. And the vision of all is become unto you as the words of a book that is sealed, which men deliver to one that is learned, saying, Read this, I pray thee: and he saith, I cannot: for it is sealed: And the book is delivered to him that is not learned, saying Read this, I pray thee; and he saith, I am not learned. Wherefore the Lord said, Forasmuch as this people draw near me with their mouth, and with their lips do honour me, but have removed their heart far from me, and their fear toward me is taught by the precept of men: Therefore, behold, I will proceed to do a marvellous work among this people, even a marvellous work and a wonder: for the wisdom of their wise men shall perish, and the understanding of their prudent men shall be hid.

There are several remarkable details in this passage that I would like to emphasize.

• Verse 9 is a strong teaching that it is spiritual drunkenness and not alcoholism that is being condemned in this passage.

• Verse 10 tells us that this is a judgement, from the Lord, upon us, our "prophets," rulers and seers. The judgement consists of blindness, slumber, and staggering drunkenness, especially on leaders. What really throws many people off these days is the fact that in many cases, seemingly sound, solid, respectable leadership are suddenly endorsing all of this as a move of God. Others may not endorse it, but are extremely reluctant to cry out against it. Now would be the "shining hour" for a group like the Assemblies of God to rise up and offer true leadership, as in days past, and soundly and scripturally take a stand against this heresy.

• Verses 11-12 teach us that confusion, indecisiveness and inability to understand have brought us to the point where even learned men aren't sure what the Bible says, even though the people look for leadership. Eventually, the Bible is delivered to unlearned people, as verse 12 says. Notice that the unlearned don't refuse to teach, they just say, "I am not learned." In other words, the time has come when theology and disciplined study of scripture is being held up as the antithesis of true spirituality and "unlearnedness" is being boasted of. As Rodney Howard Browne says,

> A diploma can't heal anyone. Place your doctorate on a wheelchair patient in the name of Jesus and see what happens. The devil's not afraid of a diploma. When you show him that piece of paper, he'll pull out his diploma and say, "Join the gang, you and I went to the same school!" The power of God is not going to flow through those who have theory, it's going to flow through those who have revelation.[1]

Is there anyone who thought that a diploma could heal anyone? What does a doctorate have to do with the devil? Is knowing the scriptures mere theory, as opposed to revelation? This is called setting up a straw man so you can boldly kick it down, and this is what these teachers do all of the time. They posture themselves as champions for "revelation knowledge" and cast those who want to be doctrinally scrupulous as dried up, highly educated, "dead heads." Jesus made no such distinction. It was He who said, *You do err, not knowing the scriptures or the power of God.* To Him, knowing the scriptures was equated with knowing the power of God!

This kind of posturing springs from an old American romantic ideal of the uneducated, backwoods preacher, who never had any book learning but he knew God! Peter Cartwright once said, "The greatest hindrance to the gospel today, is an educated clergy!" In contrast to this is the stuffy, religious, theological expert who doesn't have any faith. In many cases, this view may have some truth, but it has been taken to an extreme caricature! "Populist" preachers and prophets have almost set out a dichotomy between the Spirit and the Word! Jesus and the disciples may not have been formally trained, but they knew what the Word of God said, and weren't relaxed about heresy or heteropraxy, either.

In Toronto, this attitude is prevalent. Marc DuPont complains about the church being a house of Bible study rather than a house of prayer, as though you have to have one or the other. Arnott castigates his critics saying, "They come in here, with no power, no revelation, just criticism..." What does this imply but, "We are the ones with the power and revelation?"

Part of the problem is that many of these people are either in one ditch or the other. Either they themselves were at one time in the ditch of unbelief, "God doesn't do miracles anymore," but they came out of that ditch, into the other ditch, "I've got to be open to everything! I've had a paradigm shift!" Listen, it wasn't your emphasis on Bible knowledge that held you back from the supernatural, it was your unbelief!

But Pastor, They Worship!

•   Isaiah 29:13-14 tells us that accompanying spiritual drunkenness can be some of the most beautiful worship you have ever seen! We have experienced in recent Western Christianity a powerful elevation of worship to its rightful place. There has been a virtual worship revival that has been so much of a blessing.

But we need to begin to consider the possibility that perhaps worship itself has become an idol. By worship, I mean the services aspect of it. Christian worship is beautiful, the songs are fantastic, spirit filled groups of leaders are highly talented and let's face it, worship is a pleasing experience. But what happens to the "worship glutton" who can't get enough of that "feeling," or the worshipper without repentance? Try to understand what I'm saying here, I am a worshipper also. It is possible to get more out of the worship service itself, than to actually seek the God who is supposed to be the focal point of worship. In a certain respect, "the presence" of the Lord has become what people are looking for in a worship service. "Wasn't that good worship last night?" What do you mean by that? Can worship ever not be good? Or do you mean, "We could really "feel" the presence of the Lord?" Of course, God does often choose to manifest his presence at worship services, but whether or not He does, week after week, is no indication of whether or not you have worshipped.

Every Bottle Shall Be Filled With Wine

Jer 13:12-15 Therefore thou shalt speak unto them this word; Thus saith the Lord God of Israel, Every bottle shall be filled with wine: and they shall say unto thee, Do we not certainly know that every bottle shall be filled with wine? Then shalt thou say unto them, Thus saith the Lord, Behold, I will fill all the inhabitants of this land, even the kings that sit upon David's throne, and the priests, and the prophets, and all the inhabitants of Jerusalem, with drunkenness. And I will dash them one against another, even the fathers and the sons together, saith the Lord: I will not pity, nor spare, nor have mercy, but destroy them, Hear ye, and give ear; be not proud: for the Lord hath spoken.

God told Jeremiah that he would do exactly what the spiritual leadership boasted of, fill every bottle with wine. Now, we can see that spiritual drunkenness is a very deceptive judgement. It doesn't feel bad to get drunk, at least not immediately. Drunkenness has an appearance of some kind of religious, mystical experience. You lose your inhibitions, expose yourself, feel less conscious, lose care and worry and can give yourself over to abandonment. God tells us in Jeremiah 13 that he would dash them one against another, (I have literally seen this phenomena in Toronto, people stumbling over and against one another, to the point that children had to get out of the way.) Jeremiah, like the other prophets, taught that spiritual drunkenness is followed by an unexpected and merciless destruction.

Think of Belshazzar's feast in Daniel 5! It was at the very point in the party that the vessels of God's temple were brought out and filled with wine of drunkenness, that the hand of God appeared, writing on the wall! There are countless reports that this spiritual drunkenness is being administered to the little children and new converts. I am afraid that the Word of the Lord unto us may well be, "You are weighed in the balances and found wanting," in other words—you're too light! Doesn't that say it all?

The New Testament On Spiritual Drunkenness

Much is being made of the New Testament phrase, "the new wine." The issue of whether or not Jesus was referring to alcoholic, intoxicating beverages, in his allegory of the new life that he offers, has been much debated over the years. I think we can all safely agree that physical drunkenness is soundly condemned in the New Testament. God doesn't want His people to be dissipated, abandoned, and disorderly. What is true in the natural is also true in the Spirit. Many times Jesus and the apostles warn us to be sober, alert and watchful.

I Peter 5:8 Be sober, be vigilant; because your adversary the devil, as a roaring lion, walketh about, seeking who he may devour.

"But what about Acts chapter 2?" I hear someone saying. "If all that the disciples did was speak in tongues, they wouldn't have been considered drunken," said the speaker at an Airport Vineyard service that I attended. "Now, who all is here from foreign countries? Stand up please and say something in your own language, please..." After they all did, some German, French, Korean, etc, the speaker asked, "Did they seem drunk to you?" He then went on to tell us that the disciples must have been staggering, laughing, hanging all over each other and falling down, as in a drunken state, in order to be accused of being drunk. He failed to realize, evidently, who it was that accused the disciples of drunkenness, the mockers.

Acts 2:13-15 Others mocking said, These men are full of new wine. But Peter, standing up with the eleven, lifted up his voice, and said unto them, Ye men of Judea, and all ye that dwell in Jerusalem, be this known unto you, and hearken to my words: For these are not drunken, as ye suppose, seeing it is but the third hour of the day.

In a videotaped service from a recent prophetic conference held at Airport Vineyard, I even heard a better example of scripture being twisted out of shape. One of the "prophets" opened up his message by quoting Peter from Acts 2:13-15, but putting the emphasis on, *drunk as you suppose...* as the "prophet" progressed with his "insight" he taught that Peter was actually saying, "These men aren't drunk in the way that you suppose they are, they are drunk in the Spirit, not on alcohol." Now, this is sheer conjecture and reading into the passage something totally different than the church down through time has ever seen it, just to justify this experience. Peter is simply denying outright the cynical suggestion that the 120 witnesses of Jesus were drunken. He then goes on to proclaim in a very clear, hardheaded sermon from the Psalms and Joel about the significance of the death and resurrection of Jesus. If he had been mumbling and swaying and falling over, like many currently are doing, do you really think anyone at all would have cried out in conviction, "Brothers, what shall we do?"

Ephesians 5:18 is another passage of scripture being tortured to make a faulty point, lately. *Eph 5:18 And be not drunk with wine, wherein is excess; but be filled with the Spirit.* Paul plainly is saying "Don't be drunk with wine." Why? "Wherein is excess." Don't give yourself over to an excessive lifestyle. Don't throw away your inhibitions and clarity of thought. Rather, be sober minded, self controlled, ready to discern, thankful, submissive, and in a position to give and receive. Eph 5:18 should not be considered a parallel between physical and spiritual drunkenness. Instead look at it as a contrast, nothing is further from a truly spirit filled life, than the life of a drunkard.

Jesus on Spiritual Drunkenness

Jesus also warned much about what a spiritually drunken state could do to you. After all, if there is such a distinction between good and bad drunkenness, why didn't Jesus carefully qualify himself whenever he addressed the subject? Everything Jesus says about any kind of drunkenness is very negative.

Luke 21:34-36 And take heed to yourselves, lest at any time your hearts be overcharged with surfeiting, and drunkenness, and cares of this life, and so that day come upon you unawares. For as a snare shall it come on all them that dwell on the face of the whole earth. Watch ye therefore and pray always, that ye may be accounted worthy to escape all these things that shall come to pass, and to stand before the Son of man.

The admonition is a constant, "Be alert, watch, be sober" in short, keep a very clear head, capable of watchful discrimination.

Matt 24:48-51 But and if that evil servant shall say in his heart, My lord delayeth his coming; And shall begin to smite his fellow servants, and to eat and drink with the drunken; The lord of that servant shall come in a day when he looketh not for him, and in an hour that he is not aware of, And shall cut him asunder, and appoint him his portion with the hypocrites; there shall be weeping and gnashing of teeth.

In this passage, spiritual drunkenness is associated with people who have lost faith in the immanency of the return of our Lord. When the "otherworldly" concept is lost to Christians, all they have left to do is try to build earthly kingdoms. Thus, the misuse of men and maid servants (shepherding) and eventually partying with other spiritual wantons (hyperunity, ecumenism).

As I said earlier, over and over again, the apostles admonish us to live simple, sober, and self-controlled lives.

Titus 2:1-8 But speak thou the things which become sound doctrine: That the aged men be sober, grave, temperate, sound in faith, in charity, in patience. The aged women likewise, that they be in behaviour as becometh holiness, not false accusers, not given to much wine, teachers of good things; That they may teach the young women to be sober, to love their husbands, to love their children, To be discreet, chaste, keepers at home, good, obedient to their own husbands, that the word of God be not blasphemed. Young men likewise exhort to be soberminded. In all things shewing thyself a pattern of good works; in doctrine shewing uncorruptness, gravity, sincerity, Sound speech, that cannot be condemned; that he that is of the contrary part may be ashamed, having no evil thing to say of you.

Titus 2:11-14 For the grace of God that bringeth salvation hath appeared to all men, teaching us that, denying ungodliness and worldly lusts, we should live soberly, righteously, and godly, in this present world; Looking for that blessed hope, and the glorious appearing of the great God and our Saviour Jesus Christ; who gave himself for us, that he might redeem us from all iniquity, and purify unto himself a peculiar people, zealous of good works.

II Tim 1:7 For God hath not given us the spirit of fear; but of power, and of love and of a sound mind.

Why Judgement?

This is the difficult part of this chapter. I don't claim to be a prophet, I'm a pastor. I will attempt to interpret the current situation in the church, notably the Western, Pentecostal/Charismatic expression of the church, for whatever my interpretation is worth. Perhaps this will stimulate dialogue on the subject, if so, that would be worth it all.

I Peter 4:17-18 For the time has come that judgement must begin at the house of God: and if it first begin at us, what shall the end be of them that obey not the gospel of God? And if the righteous scarcely be saved, where shall the ungodly and the sinner appear?

- I believe that possibly, God is judging us for our rejecting of truth and the knowledge of God.

Hosea 4:1, 6-11 Hear the word of the Lord, ye children of Israel: for the Lord hath a controversy with the inhabitants of the land, because there is no truth, nor mercy, nor knowledge of God in the land. My people are destroyed for lack of knowledge: because thou hast rejected knowledge, I will also reject thee, that thou shalt be no priest to me: seeing thou hast forgotten the law of thy God, I will also forget thy children. As they were increased, so they sinned against me: therefore will I change their glory into shame. They eat up the sin of my people, and they set their heart on their iniquity. And there shall be, like people, like priest: and I will punish them for their ways, and reward them their doings. For they shall eat, and not have enough: they shall commit whoredom, and shall not increase: because they have left off to take heed to the Lord. Whoredom and wine and new wine take away the heart.

We have already written about the denigration of doctrine and the decay in the standard of teaching as well as the exaltation of experience over objective truth. "Head knowledge" is scoffed at as if it is contrary to truly knowing the Lord. Our God is a personal God and He has revealed Himself unto us through the holy scriptures and the coming of the Son of God. If anyone would know God, they must receive Him as He has revealed Himself in the Holy Scriptures, His own self revelation. One must come to Him by faith, through Jesus Christ.

The current exclusive fixation on the Holy Spirit actually could be leading people away from God. We aren't called to lead people into a relationship with the Holy Spirit. The Spirit has come, not to testify of himself, but of Jesus (John 16:13-15) To invoke the Holy Spirit as in, "Come, Holy Spirit," is not necessarily a false practice, but it can become so when the Holy Spirit becomes an isolated concept from Jesus. After all, how can you objectively test the Spirit? We know who Jesus is and what He says and does, because of His written testimony, of which the Spirit testifies. By subtly shifting the focus, from Jesus to the Holy Spirit, objectivity is removed and people are left at the mercy of their own subjective judgements. (ie "Well, it feels like the Spirit," or "The devil wouldn't want to make me feel this way," or "I have never felt so much love for Jesus!")

•   Could this drunkenness possibly come as a result of our acceptance of false prophets? I have already mentioned John Hinkle and his prophecy that June 9th all evil would be ripped off the face of the earth. In an incredible editorial in the December, 1994 issue of **Charisma**, a Charismatic leader shared her frustrations concerning the false prophecy. Her conclusion? She forgave God (?!) and said we need to pray for these very prophets, that their ministries won't suffer for false prophecies! If we pray for them, supposedly, maybe they'll get more faith. Forgave God? How can you forgive God? May God forgive us for allowing these ministries to flourish, evidently we like it, they must be telling us what we've always wanted to hear.

A major turning point leading to this judgement may have come in the failed attempt to censure the Kansas City Prophets. Instead of shutting down when their false prophecies were exposed, they were "covered" and brought into the Vineyard Ministries. Their erroneous doctrines and ministries have continued to be promoted to this day. Bob Jones, one of the "company of prophets" was eventually exposed for immorality. I wonder why the rest of the prophets didn't have enough discernment to see through his "ministry." In several instances, I have heard Bob Jones and his prophecies cited in a favourable light at "renewal" services! Though the injunction to stone false prophets is no longer in effect, the sin of false prophecy is no less serious!

Jer 5:30-31 A wonderful and horrible thing is committed in the land; the prophets prophesy falsely, and the priests bear rule by their means; and my people love to have it so; and what will ye do in the end thereof?

What Will Be the Consequences?

As in physical drunkenness, spiritual drunkenness has extreme consequences. Is there any positive reference at all to spiritual drunkenness in the Bible? For that matter, do the prophets and apostles ever think to qualify which kind of drunkenness they are talking about in their denunciations of it? Aside from Isa 29:9-14, I don't know of any other scriptures that do. I will now discuss with you (in the early stages of this drunkenness revival, while the "wine is still red and sparkling" and the fun is going on) the manifold consequences of spiritual drunkenness.

• Increased Selfishness. Drunkards are very selfish people. Whoever heard of getting loaded on behalf of someone else? So it is with spiritual drunkenness, people are becoming primarily concerned with having a "good time" in the Lord, feeling good, and their thoughts are being taken away from the Body of Christ, the lost and the poor and the needy. Shepherds who are promoting this are going to be rendered useless, sleepy, unable to bring forth the "meat in due season," and congregations will suffer for it!

Isaiah 56:9-12 All ye beasts of the field, come to devour, yea, all ye beasts in the forest. His watchmen are blind: they are all ignorant, they are all dumb dogs, they cannot bark; sleeping, lying down, loving to slumber, yea, they are greedy dogs which can never have enough, and they are shepherds that cannot understand: they all look to their own way, every one for his gain, from his quarter. Come ye, say they, I will fetch wine, and we will fill ourselves with strong drink; and to morrow shall be as this day, and much more abundant.

Pity God's flocks, they are about to be attacked by the beasts of the fields while their shepherd languish! The drunkard loses feeling and cares nothing for others, he will sell everything out for "that feeling."

• The Law of Diminishing Returns. It will take more extreme spiritual experiences to "cop the same buzz," spiritually speaking. This will take those given over to it, further and further from the simplicity of loving Jesus as He has revealed Himself. Even now, as laughter in meetings is giving way to staggering drunkenness, it can't plateau here, people will wander out further into the spiritual wilderness looking for that ultimate feeling.

- Spiritual Hangover.

I Thess 5:4-7 Ye are all the children of light, and the children of the day: we are not of the night, nor of darkness. Therefore let us not sleep, as do others; but let us watch and be sober.

I predict that hangover time is coming for the spiritual drunkards. Even as the hungover sleep in, with the shades pulled to escape the light, the spiritually hungover are going to find themselves waking out of a deep sleep, in a bad mood (condemnation), and not wanting to be exposed to any light (preaching that exposes sin). The headache that accompanies "the morning after" is also coming, and consequently these will be difficult people to minister to. I predict a great crisis of faith, much confusion, condemnation, and even resentment toward those who are sober.

Eph 5:11-21 Be not ye therefore partakers with them. For ye were sometimes in darkness, but now are ye light in the Lord; walk as children of light: (For the fruit of the Spirit is in all goodness and righteousness and truth;) Proving what is acceptable unto the Lord And have no fellowship with the unfruitful works of darkness, but rather reprove them. For it is a shame even to speak of those things which are done of them in secret. But all things that are reproved are made manifest by the light: for whatsoever doth make manifest is light. Wherefore he saith, Awake thou that sleepest, and arise from the dead, and Christ shall give thee light. See then that ye walk circumspectly, not as fools, but as wise. Redeeming the time, because the days are evil. Wherefore be ye not unwise, but understanding what the will of the Lord is. And be not drunk with wine, wherein is excess; but be filled with the Spirit; Speaking to yourselves in psalms and hymns and spiritual songs, singing and making melody in your heart to the Lord; Giving thanks always for all things unto God and the Father in the name our Lord Jesus Christ; submitting yourselves one to another in the fear of the Lord.

- Scorn, Derision, and Sorrow.

Ezekiel 23:32-34 Thus saith the Lord God; Thou shalt drink of thy sister's cup deep and large: thou shalt be laughed to scorn and had in derision; it containeth much. Thou shalt be filled with drunkenness and sorrow, with the cup of astonishment and desolation with the cup of thy sister Samaria. Thou shalt even drink it and suck it out, and thou shalt break the shards thereof, and pluck off thine own breasts: for I have spoken it, saith the Lord God.

Ultimately, this spiritual drunkenness is designed to render the church useless and irrelevant in the last days. When the world more than ever needs to see a sympathetic sober minded, Christlike church, holding forth the Word of life, what does she see? A laughing, staggering, badly deluded, ridiculous and irreverent, mystically deceived body, with delusions of grandeur (world dominion, without Christ bodily present). I believe that we will soon regret our careless abandonment of principle and allowing false prophets to lead us into error.

- Ill Treatment Within Our Own Ranks.

Luke 12:45-46 But and if that servant say in his heart, My lord delayeth his coming; and shall begin to beat the menservants and maidens, and to eat and drink and to be drunken; The lord of that servant will come in a day when he looketh not for him, and at an hour when he is not aware, and will cut him in sunder, and will appoint him his portion with the unbelievers.

What does a drunk become, but a bully? Wine is a mocker and strong drink is a fighter and who ever will be deceived by her is not wise. As people give themselves over to spiritual drunkenness, predictably they will begin to mistreat one another, speak harshly, and exercise some self given "authority" over each other. Jesus said it would be so!

- Loss of Alertness.

Luke 21:34-36 And take heed to yourselves, lest at any time your hearts be overcharged with surfeiting, and drunkenness, and cares of this life, and so that day come upon you unawares. For as a snare shall it come on all them that dwell on the face of the whole earth. Watch ye therefore, and pray always, that ye may be accounted worthy to escape all these things that shall come to pass, and to stand before the Son of man.

Rom 13:11-14 And that, knowing the time, that now it is high time to awake out of sleep: for now is our salvation nearer than when we believed. The night is far spent, the day is at hand: let us therefore cast off the works of darkness, and let us put on the armour of light. Let us walk honestly, as in the day; not in rioting and drunkenness, not in chambering and wantonness, not in strife and envying.

The New Testament is replete with the exhortation to "gird up the loins of the mind and be sober," and such like. Contrast that with Rodney Howard Browne's exhortations to "shut off the mind" and enter into the Spirit. This will only result in an increased passivity, rendering people unable to discriminate between the holy and unholy spirituality. How ironic that this happens when alertness is the need of the hour! Ultimately, this passivity will lead people into the condition described in II Thess 2:9-11 of strong delusion, whereby they can "believe the lie and be damned" not having received the sobering "love of the truth."

What Would I Say to a Person Involved?

If you are reading this now, and are saying in your heart, "I've been involved. I've been "drunk in the spirit" and have actually experienced these things and thought they were beneficial," please hear me out. God has enabled you to read this book, which means He loves you and is not casting you out! There are so many good, well meaning, devoted, Christians being swept up in this, I know that God will call us to "come out of Her" while there is time!

But it might be somewhat difficult to back out, because of considerations like this, "I thought I was "in the Spirit,"" or "Everyone considers me a spiritual giant," or even "But I've led others into this, how can I renounce it now?" Please hear me out on this. Let's consider the following possibility: **You were wrong**. So what? We know in part, anyone can be deceived. I think it is healthy for us to objectively evaluate every spiritual experience, holding it to the light of the holy scripture. You might have to eat some crow, and take yourself off the pedestal of "superspiritual leader" and admit to some people that you were wrong!

Daniel 11:35 And some of them of understanding shall fall, to try them, and to purge, and to make them white, even to the time of the end: because it is yet for a time appointed.

If you can just begin to agree with scripture that spiritual drunkenness is actually a judgement from God and not a blessing and use this all to turn to God with all of your heart, you'll be all right. But if you are proud and unable to turn away, or if you are "hooked on a feeling," and don't want to give it up, re-read the last section on consequences. Get away from churches given over to sensual experience beyond the Word. Go back to the basics, the Bible, the cross, prayer, witnessing, the baptism of the Holy Spirit, healing, the simple promises of God and waiting for Jesus to come, all of these are scriptural, this is where you began in the doctrine of Christ. Repent, go to those that you have influenced or acted foolishly in front of and apologize. Tell them you realize that this is not Christlike, that it is apostasy and you are turning from it. Find yourself a group of biblical, joyous, soberminded, old fashioned believers, (you know, the ones you were conditioned to scorn as "religious") ask them to pray for and with you, for there will be a detoxification process, I guarantee it. There will be a grieving for the damage done, influence rendered, opportunity lost, and even seasons of intense satanic accusation. With the help of sound, biblical, spirit filled believers and the Holy Scriptures, you will be able to come to terms with this whole drift away from God. There may well have to be a re-evaluation of the teachers and teachings to which you have been exposed. I know of people who have actually gone through detox times where they even wonder if they have lost their faith. Don't be afraid, you are drying out, detoxing. God is with you. If you are even concerned about it all, God is the one who has kept that concern alive in you. Just remember:

Rev 12:10-11 And I heard a loud voice saying in heaven, Now is come salvation, and strength, and the kingdom of our God, and the power of his Christ: for the accuser of our brethren is cast down, which accused them before our God day and night. And they overcame him by the blood of the Lamb, and by the word of their testimony; and they loved not their lives unto the death.

- The blood has been shed to wash away our sins, all of them, the pre-Christian ones, and yes, the ones we have committed since coming to Christ.
- The word of our testimony, do you agree with the testimony that the blood of Jesus is giving to God? *They are forgiven, all who come to God through me* (Heb 12:24) "But, Pastor, I don't feel forgiven." Well, that lust to feel everything spiritually is what got you in trouble in the first place, accept the Word of God! Out in the desert, with no goosebumps, "waves," laughter or incense, learn that we live by *every word that comes from the mouth of God.*
- They loved not their lives to death—In short, don't justify yourself or this false experience, give it up and renounce it!

Hosea 14:1-2 O Israel, return unto the Lord thy God; for thou hast fallen by thine iniquity. Take with you words, and turn to the Lord: say unto him, Take away all iniquity, and receive us graciously: so will we render the calves of our lips.

If you will do this you will find that our God is even more merciful than you ever imagined Him to be, and that believing Him at His word, is better than some cheap thrill in a hyped "church service" with false prophets.

Hosea 14:4-9 I will heal their backsliding, I will love them freely: for mine anger is turned away from him. I will be as the dew unto Israel; he shall grow as the lily, and cast forth his roots as Lebanon. His branches shall spread, and his beauty shall be as the olive tree, and his smell as Lebanon. They that dwell under his shadow shall return; they shall revive as the corn, and grow as the vine: the scent thereof shall be as the wine of Lebanon. Ephraim shall say, What have I to do any more with idols? I have heard him, and observed him: I am like a green fir tree. From me is thy fruit found. Who is wise, and he shall understand these things? prudent, and he shall know them? For the ways of the Lord are right, and the just shall walk in them; but the transgressors shall fall therein.

The Grace of our Lord Jesus Christ be with you.

End Notes

1. Rodney Howard Browne. "The Coming Revival." Page 23. RHBEA Publications.

Appendix A
Kansas City Prophets Quotes

I promised you I would give you a brief overview of some of the Kansas City Prophets and significantly related ministries. Most of what I shall include in this appendix will be quotes, to let them speak for themselves.

More Bob Jones

I believe I have a word from the Lord concerning children that would involve totally hundreds of children that would come from the loins of this fellowship...This seed will bring forth the testimony of Jesus Christ and the glorious church. These are the deliverers of the end time army...These are the children of promise you're looking upon...These are them the prophets have waited for many thousands of years to come forth...These are the ones he foreknew and predestined to come forth and to be the last deliverers of the last age...He has waited over six thousand years for these to grow up. *Visions and Revelations.*

Bob Jones on the Shepherd's Rod

So when he [the prophet] went under that shepherd rod, we saw more people leave here than we saw anointed. They were rejected from leadership cause they had flaws in them. See, that which is going to be holy unto the Lord must not have any flaws in it...it's all in scripture. When you go under it, he just turns you upside down and He looks every place on your body. And if you be found all right, He marks you to be a living, holy, sacrifice unto Him. One out of ten marked totally unto the Lord. That's a shepherd's rod...He evaluates everyone that knows the Lord Jesus Christ as saviour...When I went under at this time, He said, "There's a couple of things that's still wrong in you, there's going to be a seven month delay in your anointing." *October, 1989. Grace Ministries.*

{We all have a problem when Mike [Bickle] seeks to conjure up divine approval for his "movement" with stories of supernatural confirmations that are blatantly false. For example, Mike regularly retells the story of how the so-called "prophet" Bob Jones predicted [in May, 1983] a three month drought which would finally end with a "drought breaker" on August 23. In telling this tale, Mike makes such statements as, "we watched it day by day...June, no rain...then on August 23, three to four inches of rain!" It sounded like a pretty impressive miracle until we checked it with the National Weather Bureau and the daily newspaper accounts for that time frame. We found the following:

a.   Actual readings from the former Richard Gebaur Air Force Base, which is only a few minutes from KCF show over seven inches of rain in June, which is well over normal!

b.   The "drought breaker" on August 23, actually produced less than one third of an inch.

c.   Of the 12 days it rained in June, six of them produced records of rains heavier than the "drought breaker." One day alone had over seven times the rainfall of August 23—2.35 inches. *(From What's the Problem, Ernie Gruen.)*}

I saw intercession on a scale like I've never seen it before. I saw men crying, I saw the leadership of this entire body—one big body—all of us all over town; we came together as one big body. Men were weeping and there were prayer meetings...and because of what they were crying for, these things began to happen. We had the power to forgive sins—remitted. We had the power to proclaim liberty to those that are bound and to remove the bondage of sin." *(From "The Shepherd's Rod" Taped interview with Mike Bickle.)*

Jones' Sensual Manifestations

I was over there with Jim a while ago. My hands turned blue, and then they turned purple. And when that happens, that means you've got some incense that's gone up. You've got some intercession that's gone up that Papa's saying yes to. There's some prayers that's gone on here that the answer is yes...When you've got this kind of anointing, some of you are already entering that secret place of the Most High. You're already bowing down to that altar of incense. Your tears are falling on those coals and they're coming before Papa. Papa's saying, "Come with more. Believe for more." Because when my hands turn purple, it means you're getting through to royalty; you're getting through to the top. It's yea and amen; and that's what He's calling you into: that holy place of divine health. The Holy of Holies which your children are called to enter in can crash that threshold. It's called the place of divine health...That's what the children are entering into: they'll have the Spirit without measure, they'll walk through walls; they'll be translated—everything that was ever in scripture." *(From "Visions and Revelations," 1989.)*

[Author] Well, once you are conditioned to smell incense and judge answered prayer by the colour of a man's hand, it's only a few short steps to getting intoxicated. It's all so sensual! Ok, I told you I'd let them speak!

Paul Cain, "You Can Become the Word!"

From 1989, Vineyard Prophetic Conference.

...Every time God ever planned to do anything, the devil would get wind of it and he'd go out there and try to head it off...When he knew Moses was coming, what did he do to stop him...He killed all the babies. What did he do when he figured that Jesus was going to be born at a certain time? He released a decree through the wicked ruler to kill all the babies. Don't you see? And what's he doing now?...Abortions on every hand. So, you must know something's coming up greater than Moses, greater than,...Even in Jesus' day, because the devil is trying to kill off the New Breed. He's trying to kill off the bride of Christ and trying to kill the whole thing off, but the Lord has well planted this seed and the New Bride and the New Breed...He's about to open the womb and He's about to give birth to this New Thing...When the Word was made flesh and dwelt among us we beheld the glories of the only begotten of the Father and when you begin to become that Word I want you to know, the world will behold the glory of the Father and that's what we're waiting to see...I want you to know that we're going to have some channelling one of these days, but it's going to be channelled right out of the throne room of Heaven.

Now, the last part of that prophecy is partially true, being fulfilled at Toronto and scattered Vineyards all over the world. There is a form of channelling, lions roaring through people, even bull's snorting and in some cases, eagles. And, it has been interpreted by some to mean that the cherubim from the throne room of God are manifesting through people! Could this be what Cain was talking about?

Paul Cain's Prophesied New Order

God's raising up a new standard, a new banner, if you will, that's going to radically change the expression, the understanding of Christianity in our generation...God has invited us to have a role in establishing a new order of Christianity...God is offering to this generation something He has never offered to any other generation...beware lest old order brethren rob you and steal this hope from you. *(From Vineyard Prophecy Conference.)*

This kind of talk should scare you. Redefining Christianity? A new standard? Where does that ever get offered or promoted in scripture? This is the kind of prophet warned of in Deut 13, who is leading God's people after other gods.

John Paul Jackson

From Ernie Gruen's **What's the Problem**.

We all have a problem when so called "prophets" make completely irresponsible predictions and frighten Christian brethren with alarming prophecies...supposedly from God...warning of imminent disasters. For example, in November of 1987, after the stock market plunge in October, John Paul Jackson warns that there's going to be a fall in the stock market that 1988 will be a severe year for the stock market, and that "it will be severe between here and there, but nothing like 1988 will bring"...In actual fact, there was nothing that even remotely resembled a financial collapse in 1988. The market low was 1879.14 rather than 400 points, *[Bob Jones predicted it would go that low]* and the year closed at 2168.50, higher than it began.

John Paul Jackson on Dreams

"We can learn to interpret 99% to 100% of our dreams by recording them and figuring out our personal "dream alphabet" of symbols."

From a testimony letter in **What's the Problem?**

John Paul came and prophesied..."CCF will collapse unless it comes under "Mike's [Bickle] anointing." Two things bother me: we have done fine for four years, there should be nothing to fear..."Mike's anointing"...I want Jesus' anointing.

When all of this came out in 1990-1991, I think it's important to note, that none of these men, including John Paul Jackson, had to quit ministering. Jackson was shipped out to California to minister with Wimber. He still carries on his "prophetic ministry" to this day!

Rick Joyner, Faith Hardly Needed

From **Fullness**, Jan/Feb 1990 "The Unfolding of a Prophet." Page 13.

There will also be some new wonders coming to the church. We had some of these just recently where Bob Jones and I heard angels singing twice in a meeting. This didn't even take any faith, it was so loud and so clear, it was like a choir singing. Another time, we had the odour of incense fill a meeting for about 15 minutes. It was so intense that you couldn't help but smell it...He gave it as a witness that He was receiving the intercession from these people, the prayers and their intercession. He had said He would come with a sign that we would smell the incense. It came so powerfully faith was hardly needed. And we saw the wind of the Spirit blow so hard at a meeting you could see people's hair blowing! So He is coming a whole lot more dramatically. As one brother said, 'This hardly takes any faith, it is so obvious.' But when He comes in ways like that, it is always to give a message. He is not just trying to tickle our curiosity or our interest in supernatural things, He is trying to say something to us.

One of the major points I have tried to make through this book, is that there has been a "conditioning" of God's people over the years. They have been conditioned to become more attuned to sensual manifestation than to the Word of God. Joyner ends this paragraph by saying that "He (God) is **trying** to say something to us." God has spoken already through His Son and through the Word of God, He doesn't need to give you scents of honeysuckle to let you know He heard your prayers. He wants us to come by faith.

Heb 11:6 But without faith it is impossible to please him: for he that cometh to God must believe that he is, and that he is a rewarder of them that diligently seek him.

I could go on and on about the damage done to the Charismatic church and the Body as a whole, through the Kansas City Prophets affair, but I think I've made my point. I contend that what we are seeing in Toronto, through Rodney Howard Browne, and all over the world, is merely the logical next step, to what was begun in the 1940s, carried on by the Latter Rain/Manifested Sons teachers, progressing into the Dominion Now, Kingdom Now crowd, The Faith Message, the prophetic move, up to this day. Where is this "river" taking us? Into delusion and apostasy!

Appendix B

Note on Chapter 9.

*1. Marc Dupont's use of the lion Aslan and the phrase "He's not a tame lion." is interesting. It is perhaps of some significance that in the final book of the Chronicles of Narnia by C.S.Lewis, "The Last Battle", this very phrase, 'He's not a tame Lion' was used by the Ape (who represents the false Aslan's prophet) to explain to the deceived Narnians why the false Aslan was not acting as they remembered the real Aslan to have done in the past. (English Editor).